Don't Make Me
Count to Three!

Don't Make Me Count to Three!

A MOM'S LOOK AT HEART-ORIENTED DISCIPLINE

GINGER PLOWMAN

© 2003 by Ginger Plowman

ISBN 0-9723046-4-9

Shepherd Press
PO Box 24
Wapwallopen, PA 18660
www.shepherdpress.com
(800) 338-1445

Graphic Layout & Design: Tobias' Outerwear for Books
www.tobiasdesign.com

Interior design and typesetting by Lakeside Design Plus

Unless otherwise noted, Scripture is taken from the Holy Bible, New International Version (NIV), © 1972, 1976, 1984 by the International Bible Society.

Manufactured in the United States of America

To my parents, Chuck and Bonnie Ferrell

He has given us back the years the locusts ate.
I rise up and call you blessed.

Psalm 37:4

Contents

Acknowledgements

My deep thanks to the two most precious children a mother could ask for, Wesley and Alex, for granting permission to use examples from our own family in order to encourage others. You two are my greatest blessings!

I would like to express my deepest gratitude to Tedd Tripp whose book and video series, *Shepherding a Child's Heart,* are in my opinion, the most Christ-centered parenting materials on the market today. Your insights on biblical, heart-oriented discipline have not only shaped my own parenting, but also form the backbone of this book.

My thanks to Lou Priolo, whose excellent work in *The Heart of Anger and Teach Them Diligently* is reflected in this book.

I am also grateful for Roy Lessin. Your book, *Spanking, A Loving Discipline,* helped me tremendously to hammer out the differences in worldly spanking versus biblical chastisement. Much of the wisdom I gained from you is reflected in chapters 9–12.

A special thanks to my "cheerleader" friends, Lisa O'Quinn and Aimee Schmitt, who asked a million times,

"When are you going to write a book?" And then proceeded to stay on my case until I did so.

I thank Debra Stabler, editor extraordinaire, for going above and beyond the call of duty by ironing out the many wrinkles of this book.

A big thank you to my cyberspace hero, Al Roland, who retrieved this work several times from the bowels of my computer while I "freaked out" over the phone.

My heartfelt thanks to Glynnis Whitwer, who fanned into flame my passion for writing by teaching me how to do it right.

An enthusiastic thank you to Mark Maddox, for encouraging me to not give up on getting this book published. Your confidence in me and this work meant more than you'll ever know.

I would like to acknowledge and thank the readers who offered valuable insights for improvement: Gina Ferrell, Julie Daum, Thelma Plowman, Andi Barnes, Glenn and Lena Sollie, and James and April Martin.

I'd also like to thank my dear friend, Rebecca Ingram Powell, for always knowing just what to say and for interrupting my work with emails reminding me to "eat" and "sleep." What a blessing it is to travel the writer's journey with you!

I offer special thanks to my pastor, Al Jackson, and Patty Chance for your insights on Appendix B.

A warm thank you to my friend and mentor, Toma Knight. The wisdom I have gained from you over the years is sprinkled throughout this entire book. I also appreciate your help with Appendix C.

Thank you, Walter Henegar, for keeping me biblically correct and for *fixin'* all my southern grammar problems.

I am especially grateful to Aaron Tripp, Rick Irvin and the staff at Shepherd Press, for making this book a reality.

It is an honor to serve under such a Jesus exalting publishing company.

And most of all, I thank my Lord and Savior, Jesus Christ, for granting me the privilege of encouraging mothers across the country. May you be glorified.

Preface

D on't make me count to three!"
"You just wait till your daddy gets home!
"You don't want me to come in there!"
"Do you want a spanking?"
"If you don't straighten up, you're going to get it."
Sound familiar? No matter how you phrase them, these types of statements all have one thing in common: They aid parents in avoiding discipline issues.

All parents want their children to obey, yet many fail to get obedience. Some threaten. Some bribe. Some use "time out." Others simply ignore acts of disobedience. Could it be that parents avoid these issues because they are uncertain of how to handle them?

We mothers can tend to think that after a child's birth the hard part is over. We endured months of morning sickness, were shocked by the changes pregnancy wrought on our bodies, and even survived the life-threatening delivery process itself. What a surprise it was to learn that the hard part was just beginning!

After my child's birth, I read about the stages he was about to go through—the so-called "terrible twos" were just around the corner. I scrambled to stay one step ahead of his development. As avidly as I read "What To Expect During

Pregnancy" books, now I read "How To Raise 'Em Now That You've Got 'Em" books. As I studied Scripture and read books overflowing with biblical wisdom, it became apparent that I had to link discipline with instruction. I had to learn how to reach past the outward behavior and pull out what was in the hearts of my children. My husband and I had to make a decision about whether to spank or not. And we had to meet the challenge of just what biblical instruction was and how we were to deliver it in the right proportions at the right time. This book is the result of what I learned.

Books on how to discipline your child are a dime a dozen. Some of those books are deeply biblical. But there are few that enlighten the reader as to how to *apply* the scriptures in a practical way to training your child. That is my goal in this book.

—Ginger Plowman

A Word
From the Author

Man! No one ever told me how demanding writing a book could be. They also never told me how it numbs your brain to all other thinking requirements except its own. I believe the slang term for this condition of the brain is "fried." Recently, I actually waited in line at the bank drive-through, pulled up to the window, and stared blankly at the teller as I said, "I have no idea why I'm here. I'm supposed to be going to the post office." She looked very concerned as I drove off.

My children have labeled me "spaced out," and my husband questions why a family of four requires three and half gallons of milk. Yes, writing a book is *that* demanding. Whew, I'm finally finished. Now all that is left is to pray that the book will be used to glorify God, encourage parents, and benefit children.

I am not a parenting expert, and I did not write this book based on my own authority. This book was written on the authority of God's Word and the expertise of his counsel. I've heard many "experts" proclaim that the Bible has very little to say about raising children. Perhaps they have spent too much time earning their degrees and too little time learning the Scriptures. God's Word has plenty to say to parents if we diligently read it, apply it, and reap its fruits. Truly, God has given us everything we need for life and godliness (2 Pet. 1:3).

> "And this is my prayer: that your love may abound more and more in knowledge and depth of insight, so that you may be able to discern what is best and may be pure and blameless until the day of Christ." (Phil. 1:9–10)

PART

1

Reaching
the Heart
of Your Child

1

The High Calling of Motherhood

If I have to answer one more insignificant question, wipe one more runny nose, or bandage one more boo-boo today, I'm going to pull out my hair . . . and maybe also the hair of whoever is standing close by!

"I've had it, kids! I'm going to soak in a hot bubble bath and I would strongly advise against any interruptions. Unless someone is dead or dying, do not knock on this door!"

As I ease down into my vanilla scented-bubbles, I pray, "God, is this really what I'm supposed to be doing? I mean, don't you have something really important for me that requires a little more skill than tying shoes and cutting the crust off sandwiches?"

Let me back up and tell you about myself before I reached this point in my life. I wasn't always bordering on the brink of insanity. It wasn't too long ago that I really had it all together. I successfully managed a booming and well-respected business, counseled others in organizational skills, and drove a pretty cool automobile that would NOT seat an entire soccer team, and me, comfortably. I enjoyed television shows that were not hosted by singing vegetables or a purple dinosaur. I never found the milk in the pantry, and I never experienced the sheer panic of trying to remember whom I was calling before the voice at the other end said, "Hello?" Yesterday, I placed an order by phone. When the sales lady asked me for my address, I had to put her on hold. I absolutely could not recall my own address. It did finally come to me as I was reaching for the phone book to look it up.

What happened? The stick turned blue. I have traded in Victoria's Secret for the stretchy comfort of Hanes Her Way. I have boxed up my contemporary Christian music—you'll find me rockin' to "Silly Songs with Larry." It's good-bye 20/20 and hello Elmo.

Sometimes I feel like just getting dressed and making it through the day is all I ever accomplish. "Isn't there something more that you wanted me to do today, Lord?" Finally, I hear that still, small voice. I may not have found a cure for cancer or conquered world hunger, but as I soak in my tub, God gently reminds me of what I did accomplish today. I had the privilege of listening to the hopes and dreams of a handsome young man who thinks I'm the greatest woman in the world. He stands just over three feet tall and only gets really excited over Legos and pizza, but he is funny, charming, and never boring.

I also got to see a bright and precious smile illuminate the sweet face of my five-year-old daughter as I took time out to invade Barbie's house with green aliens. As she squealed with delight, my heart melted.

I did have a few minutes of well-appreciated privacy, as I was able to sit on the potty without someone banging on the door. I actually jotted this rare event down in my journal under "miracles." I got to read a couple of great classics. Out loud. Move over Dickens, we have the works of Dr. Seuss. I was also able to dust, organize, clean, counsel, and cook. I kissed away the boo-boos and washed away the tears. I praised, rebuked, encouraged, hugged, and tested my patience, all before noon.

Yes, my greatest accomplishment today was nurturing the two precious children that God has entrusted to my care.

Now let's talk about my greatest challenge today . . . and every day. It is raising these two precious children in the ways of the Lord. God does have an important job for me, and it does require much skill. It is my calling, my priority, my struggle, and my goal. I will rise to the occasion and accept the task at hand. I will love, nurture, and train my children the way that God has called me to do.

Moms, we need to be reminded of the awesome responsibility that God has given us. When we respond to the high calling of motherhood with passion, the rewards are far greater than any we could ever gain outside of that calling. The joys of motherhood are rare and beautiful treasures that can be easily missed if we don't seize the opportunity to grab them.

Being a mom is more than being cook, chauffeur, maid, counselor, doctor, referee, disciplinarian, etc. (just to name a few). It's about molding character, building confidence, nurturing, training, and guiding. There is nothing like the influence that a mother has on her child. A mother's influence has enormous potential to shape the person a child becomes, for good or ill.

Listen to what Thomas Edison said about his mom: "My mother was the making of me. She was so true, so sure of me; and I felt that I had someone to live for, someone I must not disappoint."[1]

Abe Lincoln described his mother as the person chiefly responsible for all he was or ever hoped to become.[2]

George Washington said, "My mother was the most beautiful woman I ever saw. All that I am I owe to my mother. I attribute all my success in life to the moral, intellectual, and physical education I received from her."[3]

Wow! What an honor! These children have certainly risen up and called their mothers blessed. How did these women do it? One thing is for sure. The mothers of these great men knew how to reach the hearts of their children. They knew the importance of God's Word in training and nurturing their little boys. They understood biblical discipline and they faithfully instructed their children in the ways of the Lord. And you can bet they never counted to three!

You probably purchased this book because you, too, desire to train your children in accordance with God's Word. You desire to be the best mom you can be. You desire for your children to rise up and call you blessed. Good news, Mom: God's Word is full of instructions for you. Let us explore those instructions together.

A Word of Warning

As we begin our journey together, I want to caution you. God's Word never returns void. This means that as you learn to apply God's Word in training your children, you will eventually begin to see the fruit. You will witness successes in your parenting. Your children will begin to change, and you will enjoy those changes. This is where a new temptation raises its ugly head. Be careful not to let pride enter your heart. Pride is so wicked that it is listed as one of the things that God hates (Prov. 8:13).

I can remember the sin of pride first entering my life at age five when my parents bought me a Karaoke machine for Christmas. I would stand in front of the mirror in my footed pajamas for hours watching myself sing. I thought I was hot stuff. By the time I was six, I was gathering small crowds at family reunions, school, and local playgrounds, singing "Delta Dawn" to anyone who would listen. I believe God knew that my ability to sing well would put me at risk of complete conceit. So, today, I can tell you with great confidence that I can't sing a lick. Well, actually, I sound pretty decent in the shower, but then again everyone sounds decent in the shower.

Proverbs 16:18 warns, "Pride goes before destruction, a haughty spirit before a fall." I didn't learn my lesson as a child, even after God left me unable to carry a tune. God didn't give up on me, though. He continuously has to remind me of my rebellious tendency to be proud, and he often humbles me. One particular lesson stands out. I learned humility well one Friday afternoon in the Winn Dixie Grocery Store about three years ago.

Normally, I do my grocery shopping in the morning while the store is not so crowded. But for whatever reason, I found myself waiting in the checkout line at 6:00 p.m. on Friday with my two children. The place was packed. There were cashiers at all 10 registers and six or seven carts in every line. In the line next to me, the very last line, waited a mother and her two small children. They were about the same ages as my children, three and five. Mini refrigerators filled with various drinks were strategically located at the end of each check out counter.

The five-year-old began to beg mom for a coke (Let the games begin!).

Mom gave a firm, "No." The boy began to walk over to the refrigerator.

Mom said (loudly), "You better not open that door!" The boy opened the door.

"You better not pull a drink out of there, mister!" The boy grabbed a coke.

"If you open that coke you are going to get it!" The boy unscrewed the cap, tossed it on the floor, and took a big swig.

Mom was screaming now, having completely lost it. "You just wait until we get home and your daddy hears about this! You kids never listen to me. I've had it up to here with you both!"

No one was able to decipher the exact location of "here" but we kept listening anyway. It's not that we were being nosy. It's just that there is nothing else to do while waiting in line, so this scene had the full attention of every customer. Now, in order for all these people to watch the scene unfold, they had to look past me and my children, who on this particular day were behaving well. Enter pride. Rather than having compassion for this poor mom and the struggles she was having with her children, I smugly thought, "You won't see *my* kids acting like that."

And then it happened. My three-year-old daughter, Alex, was standing right behind me when all of a sudden she blurted out the most horrible three words imaginable. It was as if she had grabbed one of the microphones from a check-out counter and yelled into it with all her might. Waving her hands frantically in front of her face, in a BOOMING voice, she screams, "Mama! You pooted!" My entire body froze. Time stood still. To this day, I do not know which was worse—the second she blurted it out or the minute it took for everyone to realize it was true.

I am a living testimony of Proverbs 11:2a, "When pride comes, then comes disgrace." Dear Mom, as you experience success in your parenting, please do not become prideful. Par in a grocery store!

24

2

Defining Discipline

D iscipline. Just to mention the word sounds harsh. Why is that? Perhaps its harsh image comes from the distorted definition that society has placed on it. Society portrays discipline as punishment that involves anger, yelling, and severe or even cruel acts.

Many parents today have bought into society's definition of discipline. Because they relate the word to negative training, they would rather tolerate their children's behavior than correct it. Those who do attempt to establish standards tend to miss the hearts of their children. They simply try to *control* their children, focusing only on their outward behavior. They have adopted the philosophy that if they can get their children to act right, then they are raising them the right way.

I recently heard one of the newest and most rapidly rising psychologists present his methods of child training. The television advertisement backed up his claims with a few testimonies from parents who expressed how quickly his methods reaped benefits in their children's behavior. Dear parents, we do not need the latest fad methods. We need God's methods. While some of the modern ideas sound good and may even reap some outward benefits, we are not merely after outward actions, but inward cleansing. We are after the very hearts of our children.

A Biblical View of Discipline

While society relates discipline to an uncontrolled use of physical punishment, Biblical discipline involves love, the heart, and God's Word. Because God is concerned with the issues of the heart, biblical discipline involves much more than outward behavior. Biblical discipline gets to the heart of the problem. After all, if you can reach the heart, the behavior will take care of itself. In order for us to reach the hearts of our children we must realize that there is far more to parenting than getting our children to *act* right. We have to get them to *think* right and to be motivated out of a love of virtue rather than a fear of punishment. We do this by training them in righteousness. Righteous training can only come from the Word of God.

In Ephesians 6:4 we are told to "Bring them up in the discipline and instruction of the Lord." I have found that the second part of that verse is far more challenging than the first part.

It's easy for us to tell our children that they have done wrong and chastise them for it, but it takes much more preparation, discipline, understanding, and self-control on our part to actually *instruct* them according to God's Word. This approach takes much brain activity that requires us to *think through* and *verbalize* that faithful instruction. This from a mom whose brain activity seems to be exceptionally low after a trial-some day with the kids!

When they disobey, we think we have done well to say, "That was wrong, and you shouldn't have done it . . . (*whack, whack, whack*) now, get in your room!" When we do this, we have only done half of what God has called us to do.

Certainly God has called us to use the rod to drive foolishness from the hearts of our children. We are told in Proverbs 22:15, "Foolishness is bound up in the heart of a child, but the rod of discipline will drive it far from him." But equally important is that he has called us to "instruct them." Scriptures that pertain to discipline tell us clearly that God intended the two to go together. Ephesians 6:4 says, ". . . bring them up in the discipline *and instruction* of the Lord." (Emphasis added) We see the two together again in Proverbs 29:15: "The rod *and reproof* give wisdom, but a child who gets his own way brings shame to his mother." (Emphasis added)

Fortunately, the Bible equips us in how to give a biblical reproof and how to faithfully instruct our children. We are also provided with examples of parents who successfully trained their children and the fruit they yielded as a result. One such example is the Proverbs 31 "mama."

The Proverbs 31 Mama

We all desire to be the women that God has called us to be—and we all share no greater role-model than the woman talked about in Proverbs 31. In verse 26 we are told, "She speaks with wisdom and faithful instruction is on her tongue." Where does this wisdom come from? There are several verses in Proverbs that give us clues: "The mouth of the righteous brings forth wisdom" (Prov. 10:31). "The fear of the Lord is the beginning of wisdom" (Prov. 1:7). If you desire to become a wise parent who can impart this wise instruction, you must begin by fearing the Lord and standing righteous before him. (To find out how to become righteous, see Appendix A, "How To Become a Christian.")

Proverbs 31:28 also describes children's attitude toward a godly mother: "Her children arise and call her blessed." This is not a mother who allows her children to be disrespectful or disobedient. The mother in Proverbs is the mother who taught, trained, guided, and instructed her children diligently while they were young and in her home. Now, presumably as adults, they are rising up and calling her blessed. Why do they rise up and call her blessed? Because she prepared them for adulthood. She prepared them to govern their own actions. She prepared them to order their own lives according to the Word of God. They bless her because they have been blessed by her.

Now don't expect your 5-year-old to rise up and call you blessed. It's probably not going to happen. But be patient: you reap what you sow, you reap later than you sow, and you reap more than you sow. The Proverbs 31 woman reaped the benefits of the faithful instruction that she had spent many years sowing into the hearts of her children. So will you! Be encouraged!

The Heart of the Problem Is the Problem of the Heart

The heart is the foundation of behavior. When our children sinfully express themselves, whether it be in the form of selfishness, disobeying, talking back, throwing temper tantrums, or taking swings at us or their sibling, they are drawing from what is in their hearts. Proverbs 4:23 says, "Above all else, guard your heart, for it is the wellspring of life." The heart is the well from which all of the responses to life gush forth. The behavior a person exhibits is an expression of the overflow of the heart. To put it simply, the heart determines behavior.

J.C. Ryle says, "The mother cannot tell what her tender infant may grow up to be, tall, short, weak, or strong, wise or foolish: he may be any of these or not, it is all uncertain. But one thing the mother can say with certainty: he will have a corrupt and sinful heart."

In order to understand the sin nature we must understand these three truths:

1. *Your child is born sinful.* "For all have sinned and fall short of the glory of God" (Romans 3:23). Your child was born a sinner because he has inherited the sin of Adam. This is called original sin. This explains why a room-full of toddlers do not have to be taught how to fight over a toy. They just know.

John McArthur says, "Children are born sinful, and that sinfulness manifests itself not because of what parents do, but because of what they don't do."

2. *Sin is bound in the heart of your child.* Proverbs 22:15 says, "Folly is bound up in the heart of a child." John Wesley's definition of *bound* is "fixed and settled, rooted in his very nature." It would be unnatural if your child did not sin. However, this does not excuse parents from their God-given responsibility to train their children in the discipline and instruction of the Lord. Scripture clearly states that when we sin we endure consequences. The Scriptures are also clear that parents are to administer discipline when children disobey (when they sin).

29

When parents heed God's command to train their children in righteousness through the use of the rod and reproof, God's means for driving out foolishness from the heart of the child is being put into action. God commands parents to trust Him and to take an active part in the training of their children.

3. Sin is not a laughing matter. Let's face it: Sometimes it is hard not to laugh at our children when they are blatantly sinning. However, Christians should not laugh at or make light of the things that God sent His Son to die for. Sin is not a laughing matter. We may think it's cute when little Sally is proud of herself for shoving the class bully down, even though he is twice her size. We may think it's cute for three year old Tommy to put his hands on his hips, poke out his adorable little bottom lip, and with all his charm say, "No" after Mama has told him to "Come here." But God doesn't think it's cute, and if we are to have the mindset of Christ, we shouldn't either.

Let me tell you the story of "Doug." When my daughter Alex was three years old, she knew she was not allowed to get into my make-up bag. It was dinnertime and our family was sitting at the table eating when Mickey, our little Yorky dog, came prancing into the kitchen with lipstick on. It was quite a humorous sight. Assuming the obvious, we all looked over at Alex, who began to hum innocently and act as though nothing was out of the ordinary. To say that my son, Wesley, started laughing would be an understatement. He completely lost it.

After being questioned about how Mickey came to have "Rosewood" lips, Alex looked us in the eyes and with a straight and overly serious face she replied "Doug did it." My husband and I glanced at each other trying to assess the new information. When it was obvious that neither of us knew anyone, friends or family, by the name of Doug, we turned back to Alex and asked, "Who's Doug?" She climbed down from the table and disappeared for a few minutes and then returned with Doug. Doug turned out to be a four-inch-tall action figure complete with a cape and a clip on top of his head in order that one might hook him on to one's clothes or some other item.

I wanted to make sure that she was not confusing honesty with pretending so I asked, "Alex, did you go get Mama's lipstick and put it in this thing on top of Doug's head and then help Doug put the lipstick on Mickey?"

"Oh, no ma'am," came the reply, as if she were shocked that I would even suggest such a thing. "I didn't get your lipstick because I'm not supposed to get your lipstick because that would be disobeying. I was in my room and Doug went in your room and got it aaaaalllllll by himself and put it on Mickey."

Her eye contact was quite amazing as she recounted Doug's sinfulness in great detail. She was trying extremely hard to be serious and convincing.

By this point Jim, my husband, was cracking up. I gave him and Wesley the evil eye. Jim, realizing the seriousness of the offense, tried to hide his laughter. He buried his head in his folded arms on the table, but his shoulders were bouncing up and down as he tried to contain his laughter. And it was SO HARD not to laugh. She really was adorable with her sweet, petite face, her little blond ponytail bobbing up and down as she assured us that "Doug did it."

Now we were all late for Wesley's soccer game. The highlight of Alex's week is watching Wesley play soccer. I told her "Alex, Doug did not do it. Doug is not capable of walking back to my bedroom, getting my lipstick and putting it on the dog."

I showed her in the Bible what God says about lying and told her that she could not go to the soccer game—but she

31

could go sit on her bed until she is ready to be honest. So Jim took Wesley to soccer and Alex was crying in her room because she was missing the game. I was hoping she would come clean soon so that we could deal with it and meet Jim and Wesley at the soccer field. Things are never that simple.

When I went into her room and asked if she was ready to be honest, she sat straight up on her bed and said, "The reason Doug could do it by himself is because I put batteries in him."

Keep in mind, she was three years old. I left her to think some more and when I returned . . . she was asleep. I didn't want her to go to sleep with this sin weighing heavy on her heart so I gently nudged her and said, "Wake up, Alex."

I couldn't believe it. It was like something straight out of "The Exorcist." She bolted up and deliriously began to chant, "Doug did it! Doug did it! Doug did it!"

To make a long story short, one lie began to snowball into many lies. I dressed her for bed and while I was brushing her teeth she finally began to cry. I could tell it was a cry of repentance. I asked, "It makes you feel bad to tell lies, doesn't it, Alex?" She nodded her little head. "You know, Honey, the sad way that you feel right now is the same way God feels when you tell a lie." She then proceeded to tell me what really happened. She was absolutely relieved and thankful to get a spanking. Her heart was clean.

All this to say: It would have been easy for us to laugh it off and say, "Oh, she's just three. Can you believe that she can come up with such a tale?" But God takes sin seriously, and so should we. Had we laughed it off as being cute, she would have kept that guilt in her heart and it would have hardened and weighed her down. I wouldn't trade anything for the freedom she had after receiving her spanking and cleaning out her heart. I don't think she would either.

What Lies Within

The Bible teaches that behavior is not the basic issue. The basic issue is always what is going on in the heart. "... *From within, out of men's hearts, come evil thoughts, sexual immorality, theft, murder, adultery, greed, malice, deceit, lewdness, envy, arrogance, and folly.*" (Mark 7:21–22) The "from within" part of this verse tells us that outward behaviors are only the manifestations of the real problem, which lie in the heart. The Bible uses the heart to speak of the inner you.

Luke 6:45 says, "The good man brings good things out of the good stored up in his heart and the evil man brings evil things out of the evil stored up in his heart. For out of the overflow of his heart his mouth speaks." The heart is the control center of life. Behavior is simply what alerts you to your child's need for correction. But don't make the mistake that so many parents make and allow your desire for changed behavior to replace your desire for a changed heart. If you can reach the heart, the behavior will take care of itself. Keep in mind that it is possible to cause your child to change his irritating behavior to that which is acceptable without an actual heart change taking place.

Teaching your children only to change their outward behavior is no more commendable than teaching a seal to jump through a hoop. Tedd Tripp says,

> A change in behavior that does not stem from a change in heart is not commendable; it is condemnable. Is it not the same hypocrisy that Jesus condemned in the Pharisees? In Matthew 15, Jesus denounces the Pharisees who honored Him with their lips while their hearts were far from him. Jesus censures them as people who wash the outside of the cup while the inside is still unclean.[1]

When we focus on our children's outside behavior and neglect what is on the inside, we will cause our children to become manipulators. They will learn to please us by jumping through the hoop (by acting the way we tell them to act out of a fear of punishment) but they will not learn the righteousness of Christ. As a matter of fact, if we only focus on the laws of outward behavior but fail to train their hearts in accordance with God's Word, we risk them viewing Christianity as a set of burdensome rules. As a result they may never experience what it means to truly know Christ and His power to transform lives.

God's law does demand that we require proper behavior, but we cannot be satisfied to leave the matter there. God says that we are to train our children in righteousness. We must help our children understand, that their straying hearts *produce* wrong behavior. If we are to really help our children, we must work backward from the behavior to the heart. We must be concerned with the attitudes of the heart that drive his behavior. We do this by communicating with our children in such a way that they are caused to not only understand a Christ-like attitude, but they learn how to flesh it out in their lives.

3

Drawing Out Issues
of the Heart

W e often think that if we are able to successfully express our thoughts and feelings to another person, we are good communicators. We think that if we talk to our children about God's righteous ways, we are teaching them and reaching them through communication. However, truly beneficial communication is based not only on the ability to talk, but also on the ability to listen. Let me suggest that rather than talking to your child, you talk with your child. By learning to communicate effectively, you are able to keep a finger on the pulse of your family.

We should seek to understand what is in the hearts of our children as well as showing them how to understand and evaluate what is in their hearts. Proverbs 18:2 speaks to the issue of those who only practice talking to, rather than talking with. It says, "The fool does not delight in understanding, but in airing his own opinion." Proverbs 18:13 reminds us, "He who answers before listening— that is his folly and his shame." These verses help us understand that there is far more to communication than successfully expressing our own thoughts.

The most productive form of communication is learning how to draw out the thoughts of another. When you help your child to understand what is in his heart, you are teaching him to evaluate his own motives, which will help to equip him for his walk with Christ as he grows into an adult. And as we saw in Proverbs 31, such a child will grow up and call his mother blessed.

For example, let's look at a problem that anyone with more than one child will face. Tommy and Billy are playing together when suddenly a fight breaks out over one particular toy. The typical parent will arrive on the scene and express that well-thought-out parental wisdom by asking, "Who had it first?" After going back and forth, with Mom playing detective for several minutes, Tommy and Billy finally agree that Billy did, indeed, have it first. So, Mom kindly insists that Tommy give it back to Billy.

Tedd Tripp explains the problem with this kind of response:

> This response misses heart issues. "Who had it first?" is an issue of justice. Justice operates in the favor of the child who has the quicker draw in getting the toy to begin with. If we look at this situation in terms of the heart, the issues change. Both children are displaying hardness of heart. Both are being selfish. Both children are saying, "I don't care about your happiness. I am only concerned about myself. I want this toy. I will have it and be happy regardless of what that means to you." In terms of issues of the heart, you have two sinning children. Two children pre-

ferring themselves before the other. Two children who are breaking God's law.[1]

All behaviors are linked to a particular attitude of the heart. In this case selfishness is bound up in the heart, and this sin leads to the outward behavior.

Does the Bible give exact instructions to parents as to what they should do in this particular situation? No. I do not claim to have a biblical blueprint that tells me how to solve every problem. I wish I did. But God has given us His Word and He expects us to use it in training our children. So, in situations like these, we should pray and apply God's Word as best as we can. My goal is to use the Scriptures to teach, rebuke, correct, and train in righteousness. 2 Peter 1:3 says, "His divine power has given us everything we need for life and godliness." When an issue is not directly addressed in the Bible, He has given us open communication with Him through prayer. He tells us in James 1:5, "If any of you lacks wisdom, he should ask God, who gives generously to all without finding fault, and it will be given to him."

In the situation of siblings sharing, I prayed and searched the Scriptures for how I might handle this type of conflict. I can tell you how we handle it in our home, but I can't tell you that it is the only way or even the best way. For our individual family, the most practical way we have found is to address an issue of the heart, to simplify our method, and to promote peace. Like I said, both children are being selfish, but we still had to have a "plan of action" that we could use every time this sort of situation occurred in order to promote peace. We wanted a solution that would be easy for them to understand and put into practice on their own. So, we came up with the rule that it is not only selfish but it is rude to take or even ask for something that someone else has until that person is obviously through with it.

Here is how the rule operates in our home. Suppose Wesley is playing with a toy. When Alex was younger, if she wanted it, she would just try to take it away. Now that she is older she might politely ask, "Wesley, may I please have that toy now?" If she attempts to take the toy, I usually respond with something like this:

> "Honey, Wesley has that toy right now. Do you think he is enjoying playing with it?"
>
> "Yes, ma'am."
>
> "Do you think it would make him happy or sad if you took it away?"
>
> "Sad."
>
> "Would you delight in making your brother sad?"
>
> "No, ma'am."
>
> "Do you think that it would be kind or rude for you to try to take away something that he is enjoying?"
>
> "Rude."
>
> "That's right, Alex, and *love is not rude*. When Wesley is through with it and puts it down, then you may ask for it."

We are not only training their hearts but also preparing them for adulthood. This is the same behavior I would expect from adult friends or adult siblings. Look at it this way: If I were sitting across the table from you and someone handed me some pictures to look at that you, too, were interested in, would you wait until I was through to ask for them or would you ask to take them away when I had only just begun to enjoy looking at them? Most of us would agree that it would be *rude* to ask for them before I was finished. *1 Cor. 13:5* says, *"[Love] is not rude."* So in these types of situations, I have found great opportunities to work on "putting off" being selfish and rude and "putting on" an attitude of love and kindness. These are all issues of the heart that *are* addressed in God's Word.

You may be thinking, "But what about the other child? He's being selfish, too." In the situation of siblings sharing, I have found that having a simple and understandable rule that is easy to follow promotes peace. And for the sake of my own sanity, my goal is to promote peace. I turn it into an obedience issue by enforcing this rule, and then I am able to work on one child at a time. Believe me, the sin will eventually rear its ugly head in the *other* child, giving me the opportunity to work on the selfishness and rudeness that is bound up in *his* heart.

Your first objective in correction must not be to tell your child how you feel about what they have done or said but to draw out the cause of the behavior. Can you see how that worked in the toy scenario? Rather than asking "Who had it first?" I attempted to draw out attitudes of the heart by asking heart-related questions. Since the Scripture says that it is out of the abundance of the heart that the mouth speaks, you must help them to understand what is going on inside them.

In order to understand the problem in your child's heart, you need to look at the world through his or her eyes, which is where communication comes in. Looking at the internal issues rather than just the outward behavior will enable you to know what aspects of God's life-giving Word are appropriate for the particular conversation.

Develop Your Skills At Probing the Heart

In order to help your children understand what is in their hearts, you have to develop your heart-probing skills.

You must learn to help your children express what they are thinking.

You must learn to help your children express how they are feeling.

You must learn how to discern matters of the heart from actions and words.

Drawing out matters of the heart is no easy task. It takes much practice to become a skilled heart-prober. Proverbs 20:5 says, "The purposes of a man's heart are deep waters, but a man of understanding draws them out."

Our goal in probing the child's heart is to bring him to the sober assessment of himself as a sinner, to help him recognize his need for Christ, and to teach him to act, think, and be motivated as a Christian. It is not that difficult to train our children to *act* like Christians. We have really accomplished something when we have trained them to *think* like Christians. Thinking like a Christian will help them grow in wisdom and prepare them to govern their own behavior in a way that will glorify God. We encourage them to grow in wisdom by discussing God's viewpoint in all situations. Children cannot do this without our parental assistance.

How do we develop heart-probing skills? By following the example of the King of hearts. Jesus Christ is the master of heart probing. Throughout the Scriptures, He has provided us with example after example of how to get to the heart of the matter. He was able to look past behavior and words and draw out the issues of the heart. How did He do it? Rather than just telling someone right from wrong, Jesus often used thought-provoking questions. In order for the people to answer those questions, they had to evaluate them-

40

selves. He would ask the questions in such a way that they had to take their focus off of the circumstances around them and onto the sin in their own hearts.

We all know that when you figure out something on your own, you are less likely to forget it than if someone else just told you the answer. Just like solving math problems, we learn more and understand more by figuring it out on our own. If someone gives us the answer, we become dependent on them to solve future problems for us. But if we are required to figure out the problem on our own, we are better equipped to figure out other problems, drawing from the personal knowledge gained to apply what we have learned to other problems as well.

Likewise, when your child learns how to recognize what is in his own heart, he is more likely to demonstrate godly responses on his own. In doing this, he is growing in wisdom. But when you simply tell him what his problem is and what he should do about it, you are hindering him from learning how to think like a Christian, and he will become handicapped in discerning the issues of his own heart.

Training Children To Think Like Christians

In following Jesus' example, we can cause our children to think like Christians by asking them questions that will guide them in seeing situations from God's point of view. Allow me to walk you through a scenario that will demonstrate how we can probe their hearts and train them to think like Christians.

A few months ago I was visiting my friend Lisa. Her kids, Josh and Lindsey, were having lunch with my kids in the dining room. Lisa and I were eating in the kitchen so we were unable to see them. And just when we were beginning to brag about how well the children were getting along, our conversation was interrupted by a blood-curdling scream from Lindsey. When we arrived on the scene we found out that Lindsey was crying because Josh, her brother, had hit her. At first the conversation went like this:

Mom: "Why did you hit your sister?"

Josh: "I don't know."

Mom (exasperated): "Well, what do you mean you don't know?"

As a dog chases his tail, so goes the conversation around and around. This is a typical scenario. The problem with this line of questioning is that when the only question asked is "Why did you do that?" nothing is accomplished as far as heart training.

What is the problem with Josh's response? Is Josh saying, "I don't know" because he is just stubbornly refusing to talk? More than likely, Josh is not expressing willful disobedience by not explaining his actions. He is simply being asked questions that he cannot answer. Due to his age and inexperience with discerning matters of his own heart, he doesn't fully and completely understand exactly why he hit his sister. He knows it was wrong because Mom says it's wrong and God has given him a conscience, but he really doesn't understand why he has gone against his conscience and inflicted this painful blow on his precious little sister.

The tragedy in these situations is that Mom does not see her role in guiding her child to understand his own heart. And then, not only is he punished for hitting his sister, but also for not verbally explaining why he did it. The heart training is completely left out.

When used alone, the "why did you . . ." line of questioning rarely works with children, or adults for that matter. My husband can ask me why I did something, and I still respond with "I don't know." Now don't get me wrong—it's okay to ask your child why he did something, and sometimes you may get an adequate answer. But if you ask him why he did something, and he responds with the ever-so-common "I don't know," don't just leave the matter there. Help him dig deeper into his heart to find the answer.

At this point, Lisa and I put our heads together and began to ask productive questions. Here are a few examples of heart-probing questions that can be asked in such situations:

"What were you feeling when you hit your sister?" Quite often, the emotion is anger.

"What did your sister do to make you mad?" After listening to him we found out that Josh was telling a joke to everyone at the table, and rather than respectfully listening and allowing Josh the fun of telling it, Lindsey kept rudely interrupting and trying to steal the fun from her brother by telling the joke herself. So as a response to her rudeness, Josh got angry and just socked her a good one!

"Did hitting your sister seem to make things better or worse between the two of you?" This question helped him acknowledge that he was still mad, and Lindsey was crying from pain.

"What was the problem with what Lindsey was doing to you?" Although Josh should not have hit her, we didn't want to deny the fact that Josh *had* been sinned against. We had him tell us what Lindsey was doing wrong and why it was wrong. We wanted to teach him how to identify her actions (and his temptation) biblically. There are many verses that could apply to what Lindsey was doing. One would be Proverbs 6:19 which says that one

43

of the seven things that God hates is one "who stirs up dissension among brothers." This is definitely what she was doing. The madder he got, the more she delighted in interrupting him.

At this point, we stopped and asked Lindsey, "Honey, were you promoting peace by interrupting your brother's joke, or were you stirring up trouble?" We focused their attention on what God says about stirring up trouble. We were showing them the situation from God's point of view.

"Yes, Josh, Lindsey was sinning against you, but in what other ways *could* you have responded?" Each answer that Josh gave enabled him to better understand his own heart and his own need for Christ's grace and redemption. And each answered question gave us the opportunity to use God's Word in training him in accordance with his struggle. Bottom line, Josh became angry with his sister and returned evil with evil.

Although many of these examples pertain to younger children, the same biblical principles apply to older children. God's Word is profitable and beneficial for all ages. God's Word never changes. It is only the way that sin manifests itself that changes as children get older. Selfishness, discontentment, disobedience, and other sins may manifest themselves differently with older children, but God's Word is always the same. Therefore it should always be the Word of God that we use for training them in the ways of the Lord.

In all conflicts, we should begin our training by seeking to understand the nature of the internal conflict that was expressed in the outward behavior. For probing their heart, teaching them how to think like Christians, and helping them discern the matters of their hearts, there are three issues to walk them through.

What was the nature of the temptation? Was it anger, idolatry, envy? Was it selfish or contentious?

How did he respond to the temptation? Did he respond to the temptation in such a way that God was pleased? What was wrong with the way he responded?

What other ways could he have responded that would have been better?

4

Training Children in Righteousness

I t is important to rebuke our children when they do wrong, but it is equally important, if not more important, to walk them through what is right—to put off as well as to put on. Ephesians 4:22–24 says, "You were taught, with regard to your former way of life, to put off your old self, which is being corrupted by its deceitful desires; to be made new in the attitude of your minds; and to put on the new self, created to be like God in true righteousness and holiness." Basically, we are to stop seeking after sinful desires (passions of the old self) by seeking after holy desires (passions of the new self). When we accept Christ as our Lord and Savior, we are made new in him. We are to put off our old self, our life before we accepted Jesus, and put on our new self, our new life as a child of God. (See Appendix A: How to Become a Christian.)

How do we do this with children? First, work through what a biblical response would have been. Second, have the child follow through with it. I cannot stress how vital this is in training. 1 Corinthians 10:13 says that when you are tempted, "God is faithful; he will not let you be tempted beyond what you can bear. But when you are tempted, he will also provide a way out so that you can stand up under it." When we correct our children for wrong behavior but fail to train them in righteous behavior, we will exasperate them because we are not providing them with a way of escape. This sort of neglect will provoke them to anger. There will never be a situation where this does not apply. As a rule, anytime you correct your child for wrong behavior, have him walk through right behavior. This is how we train our children to walk in the righteousness of Christ. This is what the Bible means when it says to "train them in righteousness."

Let's go back to the scenario of the brother hitting his sister. Josh hit Lindsey because she had made him angry. But the Scripture says, "Man's anger does not bring about the righteous life that God desires." (James 1:19) Josh sinfully took his anger out on Lindsey then proceeded to tell his mom what Lindsey was doing. Josh needed to take the Mathew 18 way of escape.

In Matthew 18, God's Word provides us with instructions for how to righteously handle a conflict such as this. Matthew 18:15 says, "If your brother sins against you, go and show him his fault, just between the two of you." Here we see that being a "tattletale" is wrong. Josh should have been taught to first try and resolve the matter with Lindsey in private. Josh could have promoted peace by telling Lindsey in a calm, kind, and self-controlled voice that she was offending him by interrupting his joke. This allows the offender an opportunity to repent before it is brought before the judge (Mom).

If the offender repents, then Ephesians 4:32 tells the offended child to grant forgiveness. If it works out this way, then Mom should never know anything about it. Your goal is for them to gain the experience of solving conflict according to God's Word on their own. This is how they learn to biblically govern their own behavior.

But, what if the offender does not repent? Then the offended child should knock his block off! No, I'm kidding. The next verse, Matthew 18:16, reads, "But if he will not listen, take one or two others along, so that 'every matter may be established by the testimony of two or three witnesses.'" If others are present, the offended child can appeal to them to confirm the offense. However, in most cases with children, the only option will be to move straight to Matthew 18:17a, "If he refuses to listen to them, tell it to the church," which is the authority, or applied in a home the authority would be the parents. So if Lindsey rejected her brother's rebuke, rather than hitting her (returning evil for evil), Josh could have taken his way of escape and brought the matter before his mom.

At this point, Mom said, "Josh, if you would have responded to Lindsey's sinful tactics with self-control and in a biblical manner, you would not be getting a spanking. Lindsey would be the only one in trouble." However, Josh didn't choose the way of escape, so he suffered the consequences.

Understanding the Issues of the Heart

Allow me to give one more example of how important it is to train children in righteousness and how you can walk them through that process. A while back, Wesley was going through a time where he was intentionally aggravating his sister. He would get down on all fours like a lion, snarling, growling and drooling, as he charged after her. (I don't know why in the world she wouldn't like that, but she didn't.) He would also come up with other "games" that were entertaining at her expense. I sounded like a broken record all day long! "Wesley, stop!" "Wesley, quit!" "Wesley, Alex doesn't like that!" He would stop, but then he would move on to something equally irritating. His verbal response to me was the same every time, "Yes, ma'am, but I was just playing with her." It became a never-ending cycle all day every day: "Wesley, stop!" "Yes, ma'am, but I was just playing with her." "Wesley, quit!" "Yes, ma'am, but I was just playing with her." "Wesley, she doesn't like that!" "Yes, ma'am, but I was just playing with her."

The problem was that neither of us was looking at it as a heart issue. And the reason why the problem continued all day long and manifested itself in different forms is because the outward behavior was the only thing ever addressed. He would obey and stop the particular behavior that I told him to stop, but he would just move on to a similar behavior. I saw the common denominator of each behavior but he lacked the skill to evaluate what was in his heart; therefore, he could not discern the wrong in what he was doing. I had failed to probe his heart. I had failed to draw out the sin that was causing him to constantly aggravate his sister, and I became frustrated with telling him over and over "the answer" (to stop aggravating her!). But that was the problem: I kept giving him the answer without teaching him why it was the answer. If he understood his own sinfulness and repented of it, he would be able to govern his own behavior rather than me always having to tell him to stop.

Eventually I realized that I had to work backwards from the behavior to his heart. Each time he began to aggravate her, we would go through a very simple line of questioning.

Mom: "Wesley, judging from your laughter you seem to be having a great time growling and chasing your sister. Are you having as much fun as you look like you are having?"

Wesley: (raises one eyebrow in curiosity) "Yes, ma'am"

Mom: "Is Alex having as much fun as you are?"

Wesley: (squirming a little) "Well, no, ma'am"

Mom: "Tell me, what is Alex doing?"

Wesley: (pausing for a moment and looking down) "She's screaming and crying."

Mom: "Honey, are you delighting in Alex's suffering? Because love does not delight in evil." (1 Corinthians 13:6)

Wesley: (with a look of understanding followed by a look of sadness) "Alex, will you forgive me for making you cry?"

I'm not going to tell you that it never happened again, but there was a tremendous improvement. When it did happen, I would guide him in pulling out what was in his heart. And there have been many times that he began to aggravate her and as soon as she became unhappy, he would apologize and stop the behavior on his own. He was able to draw from the understanding he had gained by evaluating his own heart. It is a process but I am seeing the fruit of him learning how to govern his own behavior through understanding his own heart. Now that I had reached his heart, my next goal was to show both of them how the conflict could have been handled biblically and without being a tattletale. I accomplished this goal through the use of role-playing.

51

The Importance of Role Playing

Role-playing is an extremely effective tool in training children how to put what they have learned into practice. When they put the knowledge gained into practice, it actually becomes part of their lives. The training will stick better because they learn how to use it in a hands-on situation. It is similar to the fact that learning all the book knowledge for a particular field of employment is of much value, but actually learning how to put that knowledge into practice can only be obtained through "on the job training."

Let me demonstrate how I used role-playing in the scenario that I just gave you. Although Alex started out as the victim in this situation, she was sinful in how she responded. As she was being chased down the hall by the ferocious lion, she cried and led the Lion right to Mama's feet. Her voice was amplified as if I were at the other end of the house rather than right in front of her. "Wesley's being mean to meeeeeeeeee!" She had become what the Bible calls a talebearer, or as we say, a tattletale, and it seemed that she would very much like to see her brother in serious trouble.

Here again is where you can teach them how to apply Matthew 18. Once again, I simply used questions to probe her heart. "Alex, Honey, have you asked your brother in private to stop chasing you?" With a pitiful face and a quivering lip she answered, "No, ma'am." "Would you rejoice in seeing your brother get in trouble?" She looked as if she were considering that question and leaning toward the "yes" end of it. I reminded her that God says, "He who is glad at calamity will not go unpunished." (Prov. 17:5)

My next step was to walk them through how to replace wrong behavior with right behavior through the use of role-playing. Rather than just telling her what she should have done and leaving it at that, I took it a step further, and had

52

her put the verbal training into practice. I had both of them go back to where the Lion first began the attack. And I put the words into Alex's mouth. I said, "Alex, tell Wesley, 'Please don't chase me and growl at me.' Now Wesley, you say, 'Okay Alex.'" That's it! It's that simple!

By having them go back and do it the right way I am training them in righteousness rather than just rebuking them for wrong. I am giving them a means of escape. I am teaching them to "put off" corrupt and deceitful desires and to "put on" the righteousness and holiness of God.

Dear parent, I encourage you to pull out what is in the heart of your child, work through how your child can replace what is wrong with what is right, and then have your child put what he has learned into practice. That,is how you train them in righteousness. Remember that this is a process. Mine will take off with the training one week and do great with it and then out of nowhere act as though they have had no training at all—usually when we're out in public! The days that our children really struggle and we become weary from training over and over again, we can be encouraged with Galatians 6:9, "Let us not become weary in doing good, for at the proper time we will reap a harvest if we do not give up."

How To Give
a Biblical Reproof

5

Taming the Tongue

———————

The tongue—God has a lot to say about such a small part of the body. It may be small but it is extremely powerful. In the book of James it is compared to a fire. As a small spark can ignite and destroy an entire forest, so can the fiery darts of the tongue destroy those we love most. However, when used properly, the tongue can produce fruit that heals, comforts, and nurtures those we love most.

The wise use of the tongue is a key component in child training. God has ordained two primary methods for parents to train their children in wisdom. They are the rod (which I will address in part three) and the reproof.

A reproof is verbally expressing to another person how they have violated God's Word. Proverbs 29:15 says, "The *rod and reproof* give wisdom but a child left to himself disgraces his mother" (Emphasis added). God has given us a balanced approach for training our children. The reproof involves the correct use of the tongue. We see this balance again in Ephesians 6:4, which says, "Fathers do not provoke your children to anger but bring them up in the *discipline and instruction* of the Lord" (Emphasis added). The discipline and instruction in Ephesians corresponds with the Proverbs passage that teaches parents to discipline with the rod and reproof. The Ephesians verse also warns us that if we do not use God's ordained balance, we will provoke our children to anger.

Someone once said, "You can spank the fool out of the child, but you can't spank wisdom into him." God's design for discipline accomplishes both. It drives out the foolishness and replaces that foolishness with wisdom. Therefore, one should never use the rod without the reproof. Discipline that is not balanced by using both will surely fail. The whole purpose of discipline is to teach children the Word of God, how they have violated that Word, and how to change. Chastising for the wrong without teaching them the right can exasperate them, provoke them to fear and anger, and fail to result in inward change. The fear and anger caused by parents who spank but fail to properly train their children can be illustrated in the training of a puppy.

You decide you want a puppy so you go to pick the adorable little fellow up when he's just six weeks old. He's so small and cute and your heart swells with love and expectations for him as you bring him home. He's going to be the perfect puppy because he will be surrounded with so much love.

He comes into your home and for a while you just can't resist holding him all the time. But eventually the newness wears off and you finally put him down, at which time he immediately shows his gratitude. He puddles on the floor, dumps on the carpet, eats the couch, barks in the middle of the night, and chews holes in your socks. The warm fuzzy feeling you had when you looked into his eyes has now been replaced with frustration and rage. You decide that you will begin the training process and that you will start with the "house-breaking" part. So you keep an eagle eye on him and the minute he hikes up that leg to relieve himself, you spank him and tell him "no." That's all you do: you spank him and tell him "no." You have rebuked him and disciplined him for the wrong.

What's he gonna do the next time he feels the urge? He's gonna slip off privately, do his business, and then cower while he waits for you to find it. Eventually you find the mess, pull him out of the corner, rub his nose in it, and then spank him again. Next time, he is even more afraid. He looks for a better hiding place and he cowers under the bed waiting for your wrath. And you wonder what happened to all that cuddle time you used to have and you wonder why he no longer desires to seek you out and curl up in your lap. You miss the affectionate love that you once shared. But it gets worse. Time passes and now when you find him, after he has left another mess, he is no longer cowering in a corner, but he is boldly showing his teeth and growling at you. You reach for him and he snaps at you in anger.

It's the same with many children whose parents spanked them for the wrong but failed to train them in righteousness. They grow angry, bitter, and rebellious. It's no wonder that they become more aggressive and direct their anger toward their parents.

Proper training for the puppy would have been to spank for the wrong but show him the right by immediately putting him outside, providing him with a means of escape. Discipline without instruction will exasperate and lead to anger. Discipline and instruction is training without exasperating.

As I stated earlier, the purpose for disciplining our children is to teach them the Word of God. It's to teach them how to change. For teaching, rebuking, correcting, and training in righteousness, we must use the Word of God. The Word of God trains the soul from an eternal perspective.

In The Duties of Parents, J. C. Ryle says, "Train with this thought continually before your eyes: The soul of your child is the first thing to be considered. In every step that you take about them, in every plan and scheme and arrangement that concerns them, do not leave out that mighty question, 'How will this affect their souls?'" Our ultimate goal in everything should be to point them to Christ.

Teaching in the Context of the Moment

Children learn general teachings from God's Word when they are in church, Sunday School, and other types of Bible studies. That's great, but don't let that be the extent of Bible training. When teaching them for the purpose of training them, don't just teach them what the Bible says, but what the Bible says about the particular struggle that they are having. Teach them what the Bible says about the problems and concerns that they are facing. Teaching applied at the moment and to the situation is teaching that will truly benefit the child. The greatest benefits come when teaching is done as you go or in the "context of the moment."

The context of the moment is the most natural time for your child to learn and grow. Too often, we try to force a teachable moment before the child is ready to learn a particular lesson. I have learned through the years that I should teach in accordance with my child's need to learn.

This lesson was clarified for me one Easter. For the past several years my husband and I have attended the Atlanta Passion Play, a musical drama portraying the Life of Christ.

Every year I find that my heart is revived, my love for Jesus deepened, and my passion for His Word stirred. This particular year was to be even more special because we would take my almost eight-year-old son, Wesley. For months, I prayed that God would use this presentation to touch his heart with an understanding of exactly who Jesus is and what He has done for him. I prayed that God would reveal himself to Wesley in a new way and that Wesley would truly surrender his life to Jesus.

The day finally came and I sat with my son at center stage, second row. My heart began to beat rapidly with the anticipation of what would happen in Wesley's little heart today. Throughout the presentation, I whispered up prayers to God asking Him to give Wesley understanding. I can say with certainty that I spent more time watching his face and trying to read his thoughts than I did watching the play.

Then came the scene where Jesus walked on water and calmed the storm. The winds blew hard, the boat rocked fiercely, and the waves smashed wildly against the boat. Wesley's eyebrows raised and his expression intensified. Suddenly, he leaned over to ask me a question and I thought, "Oh, good! This will be a great opportunity for me to explain the awesome power of Jesus!" As he cupped his little hand around my ear, he whispered, "Mom, is that a bunch of trash bags or one big tarp they are using for those waves?"

I realized at that moment that I was holding on too tightly to his heart. I was trying to force a teachable moment. As I giggled away my expectations, I breathed a new prayer. I prayed that I would be ready and willing to plant the seeds but that I would leave the timing and the harvesting to God.

Benefits of Teaching in the Context of the Moment

There are great benefits for children whose parents have learned to teach in the context of the moment. Here are a few of those benefits:

1. Children learn how to become "doers" of the Word rather than just "hearers."
2. Children comprehend better when they learn in a hands-on situation.
3. Children gain the skills of fleshing out God's Word in daily life.
4. Children are better equipped to obey God.

What does teaching in the context of the moment look like? When Johnny is aggravating his sibling, teach him that one of the seven things that God hates is "one who causes trouble with his brothers." (Prov. 6:19) You might say, "Stirring up trouble is foolish, Honey, but when you promote peace you are wise (James 3:17). Johnny, do you want to be foolish or wise?"

When Suzie responds in anger and yells at her friend, teach her from Proverbs 15:1 that "A gentle answer turns away wrath, but a harsh word stirs up anger." You might say, "Sweetheart, can you try that again and this time use a gentle tone of voice?"

When Timmy tries to get his sibling in trouble by tattling, teach him that "He who rejoices in calamity will not go unpunished." (Prov. 17:5) You might also remind him that "Love does not delight in evil." (1Cor. 13:6) And it's so important that you not only tell him what is wrong with his behavior but how he can make it right. So for training him in what he can do to replace trying to get his sibling into trouble, you could tell him that Hebrews 10:24 says we are to "Spur one another along toward love and good deeds."

When children behave sinfully, use the Word of God for verbally training them in righteousness and then reinforce that training by having them put it into practice at that very moment. So don't just tell the child who is trying to get his sibling in trouble that he should be spurring his brother on toward love and good deeds, but have him go back and actually do it. Ask him, "Timmy, rather than coming and telling me that your brother is jumping on his bed, what could you have said to spur him on?"

Timmy might say, "I could have told him that he's not supposed to jump on his bed and that I don't want him to get into trouble." Or he might say, "I could have told him that Mom told us not to jump on the bed because we might get hurt so you better get down." Anything along those lines would be good. And most important, have Timmy go back and say those words to his brother even if you have to go with him and have them re-enact the whole scene. This way Timmy is putting his training into practice, which will not only give him a better understanding of how it works, but will also equip him for similar situations in the future. This is teaching in the context of the moment. It's teaching for the purpose of doing. It's teaching them how to apply God's Word to daily life.

Keep in mind that teaching in the context of the moment is something that you will have to do over and over. In other words, you can't expect to teach them how to apply a biblical principle and then expect them to automatically have it. Just like many things, it takes practice. You may think that it sounds like a lot of time and work, and you are absolutely right! Training our children is a process. Keep on sowing and remember the law of the harvest. You will reap what you sow.

ning for the Purpose of Godliness [1]

When I was a little girl, I put on a pair of roller skates. I stood up and I immediately fell. After a while, though, I could roll several feet before falling. By the time I was 15, after years and years of practice, I could skate with no more effort than it took for me to walk. Skating does not come naturally, but through the discipline of practicing over and over and over, it became second nature to me. Although this is a physical illustration, it works the same spiritually. When we have our children exercise spiritual wisdom from God's Word over and over and over, it will become second nature to them.

Paul told Timothy in 1 Timothy 4:7 to discipline himself for the purpose of godliness. Paul even compared the process to physical training in verse 8. It's interesting that the Greek word for discipline is gumnazo, from which we get the word gymnasium. Gumnazo means to exercise or to train. The idea is that the more we train, the better equipped we become to accomplish our task. Just like skating. Through exercising and training (gumnazo), what once seemed impossible to me became an easy task. This is exactly what happens when we exercise or train our children (and ourselves) for the purpose of godliness. What once seemed impossible becomes like second nature. Lou Priolo calls this method of training "The Gumnazo Principle," and he offers an excellent illustration of how it works.

> The Gumnazo Principle can be illustrated by the example of a blacksmith who is training an apprentice. Apprenticeships are not as popular today as they were during the early days of our nation when Benjamin Franklin, for example, served as an apprentice for his older brother. Then, it was not uncommon for the apprentice to live with, be provided for, and be subject to the master craftsman. An apprenticeship

was a thorough, intense training that usually lasted for several years. Basically, it was training by practice, practice, and more practice, until the apprentice got it right. The master craftsman would likely first explain and demonstrate the equipment. Then he would allow the apprentice to observe him going through the process of making a horseshoe from lighting the forge to shoeing the horse's hoof with the finished product, explaining each procedure in great detail. After a number of observations, the master craftsman would allow the apprentice to help with some of the procedure. Instructing him, the master would allow the apprentice to try the procedure. He would correct him on the spot should he make a mistake, *and require him to do it again until he got it right.* The master may have stood behind his apprentice, holding or gripping his hands over the hands of the apprentice, as they would hold the iron in the fire until the iron had just the right glow of red. Then, *hand in hand,* the master craftsman and the apprentice would quickly bring the iron to the anvil; and *hand in hand,* the master would demonstrate to the apprentice just where to hammer the iron and just how hard to strike it. Then, he would put it back into the fire and so on until the horseshoe was complete. After a few exercises of this hands-on training, the master would be ready to allow the apprentice to try the procedure by himself. Still standing behind his student, he would observe the apprentice's work, noticing every detail of workmanship. Then, as soon as a mistake was made, *immediately* he might say, "No, this way." *Again grasping the hand* of the apprentice, he would show him precisely *how to correct his mistake.*

Imagine what it would have been like if the master craftsman had simply explained the procedure one time, and when the apprentice made his first mistake, the master said, "Wrong! No dinner for you tonight. You'd better improve tomorrow."

"That would be cruel, unmerciful, and a violation of education," you say.

65

Yet that is the way many Christian parents "discipline" their children.[2]

A child might speak harshly to his parents, to which his parents respond, "That was disrespectful!" Then the child is spanked and sent to his room and the parents think they have done well because they have identified and verbalized the child's wrong behavior and spanked him for it. Lou says

> The Gumnazo Principle maintains the fact that you haven't disciplined a child properly until you have brought him to the point of repentance by requiring him to practice the biblical alternative to his sinful behavior . . . Biblical discipline involves correcting wrong behavior by practicing right behavior, with the right attitude, for the right reason, until the right behavior becomes habitual.[3]

It is essential that the child identifies the sin and asks for forgiveness for being disrespectful, but it is also essential that he practices the biblical alternative. So after rebuking the child for being disrespectful and perhaps chastising him for it, have him go back to the scene of the crime and practice communicating the right way by using the appropriate words and tone of voice (and for many children, particularly mine, the appropriate facial expression!).

Imagine trying to teach your child how to tie his shoes without the Gumnazo Principle. Verbally walking him through the process would not be enough. You have to physically demonstrate to the child exactly how the task is done and then require the child to practice it by himself. As Lou Priolo says in The Heart of Anger, "If the Gumnazo Principle is vital for teaching such relatively simple and temporal tasks, how much more is it necessary for teaching the application of eternal truth and the development of Christ-like character."[4]

6

The Power of God's Word

The reason scripture is to be used in child training is found in 2 Timothy 3:16: "All scripture is God-breathed and is useful for teaching, rebuking, correcting, and training in righteousness." The Holy Spirit speaking through God's Word will expose the wrong, convict the guilty, and promote righteousness. In order for children to walk in righteousness they must first be convicted of their sins. They must admit that they are guilty. God uses his Word in order to convict his children. Therefore when our children sin, we should use God's Word in order that they might be convicted.

Parents with children who have not yet trusted in Jesus often adopt the viewpoint that since their children aren't yet Christians, they can't obey God from the heart. Therefore, they feel that it is not yet beneficial to train them using God's Word. After all, without the power of the Holy Spirit working, how can the child even come close to truly under-standing and obeying God's commands? And why would he even desire to if he is not yet motivated as a Christian?

It is true that the law of God is not easy for the natural man. God's law is the highest standard. It's a holy standard that cannot be achieved apart from God's supernatural grace. But that's just it. It is God's law from God's Word that teaches us our need for his grace. Teaching our children in accordance with God's Word (God's Law) points them to the fact that they are sinners in need of God's mercy and intervention in their lives. The Bible tells us that God's Law leads sinners to Christ. Galatians 3:24 says, "So the law was put in charge to lead us to Christ, that we might be justified by faith." So, every time your child violates God's law, you have an opportunity to point him to his need for Christ.

When your child speaks to you with a disrespectful tone of voice, don't just say, "You're acting ugly." Call it what God calls it by using God's words. Tell your child what God says about that particular behavior and what it leads to. "Honey, you are being disrespectful and not honoring me. It will not go well with you if you dishonor me like that. Now, try that again in a way that does honor."

The words that I have written are derived from Deuteron-omy 5:16. I used God's words but notice how I used God's words without acting like I was standing behind a pulpit preaching to the congregation. Deuteronomy 6:6–7 tells us that God's commands are to be upon our lips and that we are to teach them to our children by talking about them all day, every day, "when you sit at home and when you walk along the road, when you lie down and when you get up" (verse 7). I don't think that means that when our children speak to us disrespectfully that we demand in our most for-mal voice, "Children turn with me in your Bibles to Deuteronomy 5:16 and follow along as I read, 'Honor your

Father and your Mother as the Lord God has commanded you so that you may live long and that it may go well with you in the land the Lord your God is giving you.'" I believe that we are to know the Word of God and speak the Word of God so often in the presence of our children that it is done in a comfortable and conversational manner. It's not a formal, strict, legalistic way of teaching, but rather a way of life that is constantly on our hearts, our minds, and our tongues. Use God's Word to teach them from your heart.

When Alex was younger she went through a period where she would whine in an attempt to get her way. I would ask her, "Alex, are you asking Mama for juice in a self-controlled voice?" ("No, ma'am.") "Mama will never give you what you want when you whine. God wants you to have self-control, even with your voice. Now, I'm going to set the timer for 5 minutes and then you may come back and ask for juice with self-control." I didn't preach a sermon to her or use words that she couldn't understand. God's Word says that we are to have self-control. Whining is an issue of self-control. I simply used God's Words to reprove her in a way that she could comprehend, had her suffer the consequence of having to wait five minutes, and then (most importantly) I had her come back and ask for the juice the right way.

Once again, we can become weary in always taking the time to train them using God's Word especially on those days that it seems like you are teaching the same thing over and over. We can quickly view training them all day, every day, over and over as a burden or a trial. But James 1:2–4 says "Consider it pure joy, my brothers, whenever you face trials of many kinds, because you know that the testing of your faith develops perseverance. Perseverance must finish its work so that you may be mature and complete, not lacking anything." So according to these verses we should be joyful and thankful every time that we are provided with an opportunity to point our children to their need for Jesus by training them in His Word. If we could view all of their sinful behaviors as precious opportunities to teach them then we would be far more righteous in our training. We would be joyful and eager all the time rather than angry and frustrated. Now, I know better than anyone that's easier said than done, but we are to strive for our attitudes to be like the attitude of Christ (see Phil. 2:5).

Each time your child fails, don't view it as a hopeless tragedy. Remember that it would be unnatural for your child not to sin because, after all, he is a sinner.

I was at the mall the other day and a mom was standing in the line next to me with her two children when all of a sudden one sibling reared back and hit the other sibling in the head. The frazzled mom looked at her son as if he had turned into a green three-headed alien and said, "Why do you act like that?" I wanted to butt in and say, "Because he's a sinner. Why wouldn't he act like that?" The question is not "Why does he act like that?" The question is, "What are you going to do about it? Are you going to allow this sin to take root in his heart and grow, or are you going to use this opportunity to train him in righteousness?"

Tragically, what she chose was to allow the sin to take root because she began to make excuses for him. She looked at some of the adults standing close by and for some reason felt the need to tell us all that her son was "just so tired." "He hasn't had a nap today and he's really hungry." At this point I wanted to say, "Well, I'm tired and hungry, too, but I'm not going to slap you upside the head!"

Don't get me wrong. Conditions like fatigue can play a part in behavior with small children, but sin is sin and wrong is wrong. Even if you are tired and hungry it is sinful to slap somebody upside the head! There is nothing in the scriptures to validate the neglect of training because the child is tired or hungry. They sin, not because they are tired, hungry, or having a bad hair day, but because they are sinners. God has placed parents as the authority over them to teach them, not to make excuses for their sins.

It was also interesting that just before the child hit his sister, he was standing in line rather calmly with his mother, and someone had walked by and commented on how well behaved her children were. The mom gave a pleased and beaming smile as she said, "Thank you!" He wasn't tired or hungry then. But seconds later he is so famished and exhausted that he can't even muster up enough self-control to refrain himself from hitting his sister.

My husband and I have led several parenting classes, I used to head up a ministry in Auburn, Alabama, called "Mom to Mom," and I travel around and speak on parenting issues. Because of these leadership roles, people sometimes get the absurd notion that we are the perfect parents and are raising the perfect children.

Some time ago I kept a friend's children, and someone made the comment, "I can't believe that you let her keep your kids. I would be so embarrassed for her to see how my kids act!" My friend, April, has always been rather witty. She came back with, "What? I wasn't embarrassed for her to see how my kids act because I've seen hers act the same way!"

And how right she is. I am extremely passionate about encouraging and teaching parents to train their children biblically, but I do not teach on my own authority or my own ability because I have none. I teach on the authority of God's Word.

Actually, if you could visit my home and see my failures you probably would not have purchased this book. I am a growing parent, just like you, and although I desire to be holy and perfect in training my children, I am far from it. I strive to teach them diligently in order to win their hearts for Jesus but I'm not perfect and neither are they.

The simple truth is that all kids are sinners and will manifest sinful behavior. The question is not: Will they sin? The question is: When they sin, what will you do about it? Will you ignore them, scream at them, make excuses for them, or will you train them up in the way they should go? (Prov. 22:6)

The Parent's Responsibility

God has given parents the following responsibilities:

To use every opportunity to point children to their need for Christ. The greatest need our children have is to be born again. Our children's salvation is based on nothing we do as parents. Their salvation is an issue that can only be settled between them and God. Although we are responsible before God to point our children to the Savior, it is God who touches their hearts.

For several years, I felt that if I diligently trained them in the Scriptures, it would ensure their coming to Christ. When my son was seven years old, I realized that I could quote all the right Scriptures for every sinful issue with which he struggled and I could make him comply in accordance with those Scriptures, but only God could reach his heart. You see, he became really good at providing lip service. I would instruct him and he would verbalize all the right words, but his expression said, "I've said what you want me to say, now get out of my face!"

It was during this period that God taught me to stop relying on my own abilities. I had to let go of trying to control his heart and let God work. It was a tough time. It seemed that there was an ocean of distance between us. I am thankful for that time because it brought me into a closer dependence upon God. I sought Him with all my heart and asked Him to restore our relationship and bring Wesley to a point where he would receive my instruction with the love with which it was intended.

God led me to do two things. First, to take time alone with Wesley at bedtime each night. To not be in a hurry. To not spend that time instructing, but to simply sit on his bed and just listen to anything that he chose to talk about. Second, to go back in his room each night before I went to bed and pray over him as he slept. My prayer each night was for God to touch his heart. And He did. (For understanding how to lead your child to Christ, see Appendix B, How to Lead Your Child To Christ).

To train them to obey God by honoring and obeying their parents. We are to help them obey God by requiring them to obey Mom and Dad. If we fail to require obedience from our children, we become a stumbling block for them. *Luke 17:2* explains that it would be better for us to drown in the sea with a millstone tied around our necks than to cause a child to stumble. We are robbing our children of the blessings that God intends for them when we fail to require obedience. Ephesians 6:1–3 says, "Children, obey your parents in the Lord, for this is right. 'Honor your father and your mother'—which is the first commandment with a promise— 'that it may go well with you and that you may enjoy long life on the earth.'"

To teach them wisdom. This is applicable for saved and unsaved children. Although the Bible teaches that no one who rejects Christ is truly wise, we are still given the duty of carefully training and instructing our children with wisdom for daily life.

To train them in righteousness. Brenda Payne says, "We cannot make our children righteous, but we can train them in doing right." Paul told Timothy in 1 Timothy 4:7–8 to

"Have nothing to do with godless myths and old wives' tales; rather, train yourself to be godly. For physical training is of some value, but godliness has value for all things, holding promise for both the present life and the life to come." It is important that our children are in the habit of thinking and acting right. They need to understand that when they demonstrate the righteousness of God, they are shining his light into a dark world. This is one way they can share the power of Jesus in their lives with others.

I tried to explain the many ways that we share our faith with others to my five-year-old daughter, but I don't think she fully understood the concept. One afternoon, she decided she would act upon Mama's advice and share her faith with some of the neighborhood kids. I found her timing to be impeccable, her method remarkable, and her motive . . . well, only God can really judge the motive of her heart.

There are some kids in our neighborhood who take much delight in getting a rise out of Alex (which isn't very hard to do). On one particular day they began their war of words in order to ruffle her feathers—and boy, did her feathers ruffle. From the corner of their yard they hollered out one antagonizing remark after another. I'm sure Alex was struggling with whether or not to "return evil with evil" or follow her mama's advice and be a witness for Jesus. Torn between the two options, she pranced over to the edge of our yard, placed her hands on her hips, began to sway from side to side and with an uplifted chin, she began to chant to the tune of nanny-nanny-boo-boo the words, "You-don't-even-know-Je-sus!" Although I couldn't see her face, suspicion tells me that she stuck out her tongue after the chant. Needless to say, we're still working on how to share our faith.

74

"Joan" The Baptist

Besides the Proverbs 31 woman, I view my responsibility as being most like that of John the Baptist. Let me explain. We as parents are given the awesome responsibility of standing in the gap for our children. Before they surrender to the Lordship of God and come under His authority, they are sovereignly under the only authority they know—their parents. This divine era places us in the gap between God and our children. God has called us to be "John the Baptist" for our children. In obedience to the call of God, John devoted his life to preparing the way for Jesus. God used John's words and actions to help prepare those whom Jesus would later call to himself.

In the same way, God has entrusted us to prepare the hearts of our children for the Savior. We are tools used by God to whittle away the calluses of the heart, keeping the heart tender and inclined to obedience. When we call our children to obey us we are preparing them to obey Jesus, which is our ultimate goal. When they accept Jesus and surrender to His Lordship, they find it easier to heed His commands because they are already in the habit of obeying. Let's go before the Lord just as John the Baptist did and "prepare the way."

To pray for them. We should bathe all of our efforts in prayer for our children's salvation. We can obey God by training and instructing our children, but it is God who changes their hearts. (For learning how to pray for your children, see Appendix C, How to Pray For Your Children)

To be a godly example. We are to teach by our example. Many years ago my friend Toma wrote me a note that said, "Your talk talks and your walk talks but your walk talks more than your talk talks."

J. Vernon McGee tells a story about a father who kept a jug of whiskey out in the corncrib in the barn. Every morning he was in the habit of going out and getting himself a swig of whiskey. One morning, he headed out to the barn, as was his habit, but this time he heard someone behind him. He turned around and found that it was his little son following him, stepping in the footsteps in the snow where his father had walked. The father asked, "What are you doing, Son?" The boy answered, "I'm following in your footsteps." The father sent the boy back into the house, went out to the corncrib, and smashed the bottle of whiskey.

Someone is following in your footsteps. Your child learns the most not by what he hears you say but by what he sees you do. He will follow many of the examples that you set before him. In following your example, will he be a doer of the Word of God or only a hearer? Will he be faithful or hypocritical? Perhaps one of the most sobering verses as far as our responsibility in training our children is found in Luke 6:40: "A student is not above his teacher, but everyone who is fully trained will be like his teacher."

Why Do I Reprove My Children?

In Matthew 18:15 God commands that we reprove those who are caught in sin. Reproving our children in accordance with the Scriptures exposes the wrong by shedding light where there is darkness, thus convicting the guilty person. Now let me clarify one point. We are simply the vehicles delivering the Word of God. It is God's Word and God's Spirit that actually convicts.

When To Reprove Children

How do I know when I should reprove my children?

When your child has sinned. A reproof is in order whether your child sins intentionally or unintentionally.

Before you administer a spanking. You should never spank your child without telling him exactly what he has done wrong and what he can do to make it right.

Although a reproof should always accompany biblical chastisement, sometimes a reproof alone is all that is needed. Here are two kinds of situations in which a reproof alone should be given:

When the child has not been informed of the parent's standard. That is, he did not know that what he was doing was wrong or disobedient. In order for our children to understand their responsibilities in abiding by the standards, we have to communicate those standards to them. One way to do this is by discussing the standard during times of non-conflict. There are many ways to do this. You can purchase character development devotionals or study Bible characters together. There are plenty of Bible based books for kids that give examples of how to demonstrate godly character in various situations. Children are quicker to absorb moral lessons during times that they are not in trouble. Another way to help your children abide by the standard is to discuss what is expected before going into a situation where you know they will be tempted to disobey.

For example, while traveling to the grocery store, you might ask your children, "Who knows what you are *not* supposed to do while in the grocery store?" When my children were younger, we would actually make a "game" out of it. They got a "point" for each answer. Their responses might include: "We are not supposed to touch things on the shelves. We are not supposed to ask for a bunch of 'junk.' We are not supposed to walk away from you."

After they had accepted responsibility for what *not* to do, I would ask, "Who knows what you *should* do in the grocery store?" Their responses might include: "We should walk beside you. We should speak when spoken to. We should not 'hang' on the buggy."

Not only does training in times of non-conflict give them a clear understanding of what is expected, but it also aids in preventing disobedience.

When the child is not characterized by the sin in which he was caught. In other words, let's say that your child knows that it is your standard that he comes to you as soon as you call him and for some time now, he has been characterized by responding promptly to your call and immediately coming to you. Let's say that one afternoon you call him and he yells, "I'm busy, Mom." This is not the time to chastise him because he is not characterized by disobeying you in this area. This is when you should demonstrate grace, just as our Lord demonstrates grace, and simply reprove him. Now, if he does it again the next day, chastisement would be in order.

CHAPTER

7

Managing the Manipulator

An often overlooked sin that warrants reproof is manipulation. Lou Priolo defines manipulation as "an attempt to gain control of another individual or situation by inciting an *emotional reaction* rather than a *biblical response* from that individual . . . For a Christian, manipulation is using unbiblical means for controlling or influencing another person" (Emphasis added).[1]

I personally believe that women are better at manipulating than men, even as children. Take my daughter, Alex. She is a prime example of a young woman's mind at work.

I had run several errands with Alex and her friend, Molly, age four. As we approached the car one last time, I prepared myself to handle the conflict that I had avoided each time the girls had entered the car: who got to climb in first. I opened the back door and, once again, the girls pushed their way past my legs to see who could be the first one in. But before I could offer my counsel for resolving the conflict once and for all, Alex spoke up and said, "Molly, this time I am going to be kind and generous." I glanced down at her sincere little face and thought to myself, "Praise the Lord." Then she continued, "This time I am going to get in first because I want to be kind." Four-year-old Molly looked puzzled. With a scrunched up nose and raised upper lip Molly asked, "Huh?" Alex's matter-of-fact reply came as she dove in before her friend, "Molly, don't you know that the first will be last and I don't want you to be last so I'm getting in first!"

See what I mean? Girls have the ability to get what they want and still make the other person feel that they came out on top. It's really quite amazing if you think about it.

What about boys? Oh yeah, they have their natural abilities as well.

It's late at night when you hear a ruckus coming from the kitchen. It sounds much like the popping of the glass cookie jar lid. You suspiciously tiptoe to the crime scene and then barge in through the swinging door. Your wide-eyed little "dear" looks as if he has been caught in the headlights. He's caught all right, but his quick and clever antics reach way beyond that of a typical three-year-old. As you temporarily experience the loss of common sense, you firmly ask, "What are you doing, Son?" The chubby little arm extends, offering you the cookie as he sweetly replies, "I was getting a cookie for you, Momm . . . may I have one, too?"

The Younger Manipulator

Manipulation is easier to detect in younger children than in older children. Younger children may cry, whine, beg, or throw a temper tantrum in order to attain whatever it is that they want. When they do this they are *acting foolishly*. And when Mom rewards the child's sinful attempt for personal gain by giving him what he wants, she is *responding foolishly*.

The Older Manipulator

Older manipulators were once younger manipulators who have just sharpened their tactics. Their tactics used to be an obvious attempt to gain control of the other person or the situation. Now their attempts are a little more clever, making them more subtle and harder to detect. Older children may accuse, criticize, pout, ask "Why?" questions, give you the cold shoulder, or withhold affection in order to manipulate your response. When they do this they are *acting foolishly*. Mom may reward the child's sinful attempt for personal gain by defending herself, justifying her actions, blame-shifting, answering the "Why?" questions, or arguing. When Mom does this she is *responding foolishly*.

Responding to Manipulation

God has given parents instructions for how to respond to manipulation:

"Do not answer a fool according to his folly, lest you also be like him. Answer a fool as his folly deserves, lest he be wise in his own eyes." (Prov. 26:4-5) This is not to say that children are fools but that they are capable of acting foolishly and in accordance with their sinful nature. The genius of God's wisdom in this proverb is that it accounts for different kinds of foolishness. If a child is stubbornly clinging to a particularly foolish justification for his actions, parents should avoid being drawn into endless argument and, if necessary, move directly to discipline. But if your child shows signs of teachability, you can graciously rescue him from the folly of being "wise in his own eyes."

The Bible gives us many examples of people, both friends and enemies, who tried to manipulate Jesus. Jesus never answered a foolish question or accusation with a foolish response. Instead, he responded in such a way that the fool was unable to walk away from the conversation believing that he was "wise in his own eyes." Many times Jesus showed the fool His own foolishness by causing him to evaluate his own heart. Jesus did this by turning the focus away from the manipulative remark and onto the manipulator's own heart and motives.

For example, Luke chapter 10 recounts the time when Jesus came into the home of Mary and Martha. Mary sat at the Lord's feet and listened to his words, while Martha was distracted by all the preparations that had to be made for the guests. Now, what Martha wanted was assistance in helping with the preparations, but rather than simply asking for help, she tried to manipulate Jesus into making Mary help. In Luke 10:40 Martha whines, "Lord, don't you care that my sister has left me to do all the work myself? Tell her to help me!" Jesus responded in such a way that Martha had to take her focus off of what Mary was doing and onto the motives of her own heart. In verses 41–42 Jesus responded, "Martha, Martha, you are worried and upset about many things, but only one thing is needed. Mary has chosen what is better, and it will not be taken away from her" (Emphasis added).

At other times, Jesus thwarted his manipulators' intentions by avoiding their questions altogether, thus demonstrating their foolishness to the crowd. For example, in Matthew 21:23–28, the chief priests and elders questioned Jesus' authority in order to undermine his ministry in front of the crowd.

Instead of defending himself and inciting the controversy they sought, he posed a question that exposed their own enslavement to popular opinion: "John's baptism—where did it come from? From heaven, or from man?" (verse 25). When they refused to answer the question, Jesus responded, "Neither will I tell you by what authority I do these things." (verse 28)

Our responsibility is to respond to foolishness the same way as Jesus did. As parents, we can judge the words and actions of our children but we do not have the ability to judge their thoughts and motives. However, if we are wise we can help them to evaluate what is in their own heart. We can guide them in pulling out the foolishness that is bound up there. Here are a few examples of how this might work:

Example #1

How are you going to respond?

Your daughter is having a great time playing "dress up" in her room. You tell her that she can play for five more minutes and then she needs to clean up her room because it's time for lunch. In a whiney voice she says, "But whyyyyyy?" Let me add that there are two kinds of "why" questions. There is the "why?" that is used to manipulate, and there is the sincere "why?" that really seeks an answer. It's usually not hard to discern between the two. Mom had already said it was time for lunch. Obviously, the whiney "why?" question is an attempt to manipulate Mom into allowing her to keep playing.

> A. You can answer her according to her folly and say, "Because you have been playing for an hour and I just told you that it's time for lunch."

B. You can answer her as her folly deserves and say, "Honey, could it be that you are more interested in playing 'dress up' than pleasing the Lord? God says, "Children obey your parents in everything, for this pleases the Lord" (Col. 3:20).

Example #2

How are you going to respond?

Your son is outside playing with a neighborhood friend. You tell him that he needs to tell his friend goodbye because it is time for his haircut appointment. With a disgruntled face he says, "You never let me play with Jimmy. I don't ever get to have any fun!"

A. You can answer him according to his folly and say, "Yes you do get to have fun and I let you play with Jimmy three days ago!"
B. You can answer him as his folly deserves and say, "Could it be that you are trying to make me feel guilty in order to get what you want? You should desire to honor and obey your parents more than you desire to play outside with Jimmy. Son, be careful to not become a lover of pleasure more than you are a lover of God." (Prov. 21:17; 2 Timothy 3:4)

8

Guidelines for Verbal Correction

I can relate to the frustrations of parenting little ones all day. Been there, done that! I also know how easy it is for mom to lose her cool. I was really struggling one day in particular when my children were younger. Feeling guilty for the harsh words and not-so-sweet tone of voice I had used all day, I decided to write down some guidelines that would enable me to keep myself in check. Perhaps you might benefit from them as well.[1]

Guideline #1: Examine your motives. Am I doing this because my will has been violated or God's will has been violated? Am I correcting my child because he has sinned against God or because his behavior has caused me some personal discomfort, embarrassment, or trouble?

Consider another personal example. This is the Sunday that you arrive in church after a less-than-pleasant morning, only to find that the only seats available are on the first row, squarely in front of the pastor and choir. You reluctantly arrange your family in a "most likely to succeed" format. It's not working. They begin to wiggle and squirm as if their breakfast consisted of nothing but Tootsie Rolls and M&M's. They start out with this little head-bobbing thing. Then they scoot up to the edge of the pew and progress into the full body rock, swaying from side to side with glazed-over eyes. Some sort of gurgle noise that doesn't sound human begins to sound in beat with the body rock. By the middle of the service and after several stern warnings and threats, they are lying down backwards in the pew with their feet sticking straight up in the air. You turn to mouth an apology to the people behind you and find them staring at your children with an annoyed look on their faces. By the end of the service, you have already vented a little anger by informing them through clenched teeth of what is going to happen to them when they get home. So, now they are whimpering and whining rather loudly, "BUT I DON'T WANT A SPAAAANKIIIIING." By the time you get to the foyer, they have completely lost it. They have fallen out on the floor, kicking and screaming, and you are dragging them out by one leg. It is times such as these that you need to pray through your motives before you administer any form of discipline.

Our children can sense when they are being violated by impure motives, and God knows the motives of our hearts. If our motive is sinful, we will give reproof in a sinful way and our children will view it as a personal attack or an act of vengeance. This may result in them becoming angry rather than repentant. Pray through your motives before you reprove your child if you feel that they are in question.

For example, nothing irritates me more than when I am talking to an adult and one of my children interrupts our conversation. However, if I am motivated by sinful anger, I will sin against God and my child when I administer a reproof. My motive should not be revenge because I am irritated or inconvenienced. My motive should be to drive out the rudeness and inconsiderate disrespect from the heart of my child. If my motive is sinful I might say, "I can't believe you are so inconsiderate. I am trying to talk to her and you are acting so ugly!" But if my motive is righteous rather than selfish I might say, "Honey, do you think it is kind or rude for you to interrupt Mama while she was talking to someone? Are you thinking about others or yourself when you interrupt? What could you have done rather than interrupting?" Always remember to apply Galatians 6:1 when reproving your child: "Brothers, if someone is caught in sin, you who are spiritual should restore him *gently*" (Emphasis added).

Also, remember that we are to provide our children with a means of escape rather than just rebuking them for wrong. "No temptation has seized you except what is common to man. And God is faithful; he will not let you be tempted beyond what you can bear. But when you are tempted, he will also provide a way out so that you can stand up under it." (1 Cor. 10:13) Children often feel the sudden urge to communicate something to Mom while she is speaking with someone else. To prevent rude interruptions, our children are required to place their hand on me and wait for me to give them permission to speak. This way, they are not exasperated. After all, when two mommies are talking it can seem like an eternity before there's a pause in the conversation. This can seem unbearable to a small child.

When my children place their hand on my arm (or wherever) they are letting me know in a way that shows respect for me and the other person, "Mom, I need to say something but I don't want to be rude." I will usually place my hand on top of theirs to communicate, "I know you need something, and I'll ask you as soon is there is a pause in conversation." As soon as it is convenient, I will give them permission to talk. This is providing them with a means of escape. Teaching them to put their hand on you rather than interrupting is not a biblical mandate. It is a tool, used to prevent exasperation.

Guideline #2: Examine your life. Have I provoked my child in some way? What is my example? How do I act when things don't go my way? Have I led my child into sin by failing to teach him? By failing to provide him with a means of escape? By failing to train him in what is right? Have I given my child more freedom than he can handle? We should apply the biblical admonition: "You hypocrite, first take the plank out of your own eye, and then you will see clearly to remove the speck from your brother's eye." (Matt. 7:5)

Guideline #3: Choose the right time and place. Do not embarrass your child. He will be more attentive to your instructions if he is not embarrassed because of being reproved in front of his friends. When you reprove your child in front of others, you take his focus off of the sin in his heart and onto the embarrassment and humiliation that you have unnecessarily caused him. Your goal is not to embarrass him but to bring him to repentance. Occasionally it may be necessary to reprove your child in front of others but most of the time, if others are around, it would be better to take the child into another room or quietly instruct him in his ear. Jesus taught us, "If your brother sins go and reprove him in private; if he listens to you, you have won your brother" (Matt. 18:15).

Guideline #4: Choose the right words. Be careful not to replace God's wisdom with man's wisdom. Rather than using worldly terminology, use biblical terminology. For example, when speaking to your child, don't substitute:

"You are being disrespectful" with "You are acting ugly."
"Telling a lie" with "Telling a fib."
"Being foolish" with "Being stubborn."
"Being disobedient" with "Being strong-willed."

Use biblical terminology when you can because it is the power of God's words and God's wisdom that will truly penetrate the hearts of your children. Hebrews 4:12 explains this power clearly: "The Word of God is living and active; sharper than a double edged sword; it penetrates even to dividing soul and spirit, joints and marrow; it judges the thoughts and attitudes of the heart."

Guideline#5: Choose the right tone of voice. Make a conscious effort not to scold your child. You are ready to reprove your child biblically when you can speak to him in a normal tone of voice and with carefully measured words: "The heart of the righteous weighs its answers but the mouth of the wicked gushes evil" (Prov. 15:28). Back in 1891, H. Clay Trumbull wrote about the dangers of scolding:

Scolding is, in fact, never in order, in dealing with a child, or any other duty in life. To "scold" is to assail or revile with boisterous speech . . . Scolding is always an expression of a bad spirit and of a loss of temper . . .

If a child has done wrong, a child needs talking to; but no parent ought to talk to a child while that parent is unable to talk in a natural tone of voice, and with carefully measured words. If the parent is tempted to speak rapidly, or to multiply words without stopping to weigh them, or to show an excited state of feeling, the parent's first duty is to gain entire self-control. Until that control is secured, there is no use of the parent's trying to attempt any measure of child training. The loss of self-control is for the time being an utter loss of the power for the control of others. . . .

If, indeed, scolding has any good effect at all, that effect is on the scolder, and not the scolded. Scolding is the outburst of strong feeling that struggles for the mastery under the pressure of some outside provocation. It never benefits the one against whom it is directed, nor yet those who are its outside observers, however, it may give physical relief to the one who indulges in it. If, therefore, scolding is an unavoidable necessity on the part of any parent, let that parent at once shut himself, or herself, up, all alone, in a room where the scolding can be indulged in without harming anyone. But let it be remembered that, as an element in child training, scolding is never, never in order.[2]

Allow me to illustrate the difference between scolding and biblically reproving. It was a cold day in February. My children asked if they could go outside to play. I gave them permission to go out but only after they had put on their coats and shoes.

Now, you have to understand that my daughter, Alex, absolutely delights in being barefooted. As she whizzed by, I confirmed my orders by repeating, "Don't forget to put on your shoes."

Twenty minutes passed. Then, as I was taking out the trash, what should I find but Alex, running around on bare feet that had turned a bluish purple color. As if that wasn't enough to light my fire, her new pants were a little too long for her legs so without her shoes she stepped on them. After grinding the bottom of her pants into the concrete for twenty minutes, she now had two holes in them. It may have been cold outside, but the heat building up in Mama at that moment could have warmed the entire neighborhood.

Alex had directly disobeyed me. There are two ways that I could respond:

I could scold her. I could harshly say, "Alex, I TOLD you to put your shoes on! Now your feet are HALF FROZEN and just LOOK at what you have done to your pants! (With hands on hips and finger wagging frantically) YOUR DADDY works so hard to buy you these clothes, and THIS is how you show your appreciation! You just see how fast you can get your tail in your room! You are getting a major spanking, young lady!"

I could biblically reprove her in love. I can gently say, "Alex, Honey, I told you to put on your shoes before you went out. Have you obeyed or disobeyed Mama?" After she verbalizes that she has disobeyed, I can come back with, "Well, Sweetheart, God says that children are to obey their parents. Mama loves you too much to allow you to disobey. Now, go to your room and I'll be in there in just a minute."

To which response do you think she will be more receptive? Which one shows unconditional love and careful instruction? Which one will she learn from without being provoked to anger? Remember that scolding is an angry response. "A gentle answer turns away wrath but a harsh word stirs up anger." (Prov. 15:1)

If you struggle with your tone, as I do, rather than reproving your child in a normal tone of voice you can even try and soften your voice a little when you are giving a reproof. When I am in the habit of making a conscious effort to instruct my children in a softer voice than I normally use, it helps me to have self-control.

Guideline #6: Be prepared to suggest a biblical solution. This is what we talked about earlier. We can tell our children what to put off (sinfulness) but we must remember that it is even more important to tell them what to put on (righteousness), to train them in how to replace that wrong behavior with right behavior, and to then have them actually exercise what they have learned. The Bible describes it this way: "You were taught, with regard to your former way of life, to put off your old self, which is being corrupted by its deceitful desires; to be made new in the attitude of your minds; and to put on the new self, created to be like God in true righteousness and holiness." (Eph. 4:22–23)

A Place for Anger in Reproof

"My dear brothers, take note of this: Everyone should be quick to listen, slow to speak, and slow to become angry, for man's anger does not bring about the righteous life that God desires." (James 1:19–20)

Understand that all anger is not sinful. The Bible does not say, "Do not become angry." It does say, "In your anger, do not sin." (Eph. 4:26) Anger is an emotion given to us by God. There is a difference between sinful anger and righteous anger. Ask yourself, "Am I angry because my will was violated (sinful anger) or because God's will was violated (righteous anger)?" However, even if our anger is righteous, we must be careful to not express that anger using sinful forms of communication such as screaming, throwing things, or name-calling.

When is Anger Sinful?

Anger is sinful when:

It outwardly attacks another. Sinful anger may say, "I told you to stand beside me in the store! What's the matter with you! Why can't you just do what I say!" Righteous anger may say, "Honey, I told you to stand beside me in the store. Did you obey or disobey? That's right, you disobeyed and I love you too much to allow you to disobey."

It dwells within the heart. When anger is not dealt with biblically it becomes resentment and bitterness. This sinful anger may manifest itself by holding grudges, giving your child the silent treatment or the cold shoulder. Righteous

92

anger works on the child's heart and deals with the sin through communicating God's Word and heeding His commands when it comes to discipline.

By training our children in righteousness using God's Word, we are preparing them to govern their own actions and enabling them to discern matters of their own hearts. We want them to heed our instructions so that they can learn how to discern what is right.

Proverbs 17:10 reminds us that "A rebuke impresses a man of discernment more than a hundred lashes a fool."

Wise Words for Moms and Dads

I have spent a great deal of time in the previous chapters talking about how important it is to reach the heart of your child and reprove your child using the Word of God. For some of you, this all might be very new. If you are not experienced in training your children in accordance with the Scriptures, then all of this has probably been a little overwhelming to you. You may be thinking, "I wouldn't have a clue as to how to go about finding out which scripture to use for different struggles my kids are having. I wouldn't even know where to start."

Good news! I have developed a "Wise Words for Mom" chart to give you a boost.[3]

The following chart was designed for Moms, but it is useful for Dads as well.

*"The heart of the righteous studies
how to answer."*
Proverbs 15:28

93

Wise Words for Mom

Child's Behavior	Heart Probing Question	Reproof ("Put Off")	Encouragement ("Put On")	Additional Verses
Aggravating, Stirring Up Strife, Picking on Others	1. Are you purposing in your heart to promote peace, or are you stirring up trouble? 2. How can you show love and pursue peace in this situation?	**Strife.** One of the seven things God hates is one who stirs up trouble among his brothers. Proverbs 6:19	**Peace Making.** God gives joy to those who promote peace. 1 Peter 3:11 Proverbs 12:20	*1 Peter 3:11* *Proverbs 10:12* *Proverbs 12:20*
Bad Friendships	1. Do you think this friend will encourage you to follow Jesus? 2. Do you think it is a wise decision to "hang out" with this person? *NOTE:* Be careful not to condemn the foolish but pray for them out of love and compassion.	**Bad** Company. You should stay away from those whose ways are contrary to the teaching you have learned or you will be led astray and suffer harm. Romans 16:17, Proverbs 12:26, Proverbs 13:20	**Wisdom.** If you walk with the wise you will grow wise. Proverbs 13:20	*Proverbs 22:24–25* *Proverbs 28:26* *Romans 16:17*
Blame Shifting, Making Excuses	1. Could it be that you are trying to **cover** over your own sin? 2. Without blaming someone else or making excuses, I want you to examine your own heart and tell me what you did. 3. What could you have done differently?	**Pride.** When you try to hide your sins you will not prosper. God knows what is in your heart. Proverbs 28:13	Humility. If you confess and turn away from your sin, you will be forgiven and will receive mercy. Proverbs 28:13, 1 John 1:9	*Proverbs 21:2* *Micah 7:9* *James 5:16*

Bragging, Conceit	Do those words bring glory and honor to God or to yourself?	**Pride.** "Let another praise you, and not your own mouth; someone else, and not your own lips." (*Proverbs 27:2*) God will not tolerate a proud heart. Psalm 101:5	**Humility.** Walk in humility and consider others better than yourself. Philippians 2:3	*1 Samuel 16:7b* *Romans 12:3* *1 Corinthians 1:31* *Galatians 6:14*
Complaining	1. Is your attitude showing thankfulness and contentment? 2. Rather than complaining, what can you be thankful for in this situation?	**Complaining.** "Do everything without complaining and arguing." (*Philippians 2:14*)	**Thankfulness.** It is God's will that you be thankful and joyful in all circumstances. 1 Thessalonians 5:16–18	*Proverbs 17:22* *Colossians 3:17, 23*

How to use this chart

This chart was designed for the purpose of aiding you in using the Scriptures to drive out the foolishness "bound up in the heart of [your] child" (Proverbs 22:15). It does not contain everything you need to know about the sinful behaviors that are listed, nor does it contain every sinful behavior that you may come up against. Therefore, it should be used as a tool—not a substitute—for your personal research of the Bible when it comes to teaching, rebuking, correcting, and training your children in righteousness.

PART

3

The Biblical Use of the Rod

CHAPTER

9

The Tailbone's Connected to the . . . Heart?

M any parents today are perplexed over the issue of whether or not to spank their children. Some say that it is a cruel and abusive form of punishment, or that it promotes violence. Others simply say that they "Don't believe in spanking." Even some well-respected Christian child psychologists advise against spanking. It's easy to become confused.

Let's look at these arguments first. The first two may have some validity. Certainly, there are homes where the parents spanked and the child grew up with a bent toward violence. However, in most of these cases, the parents had embraced a worldly form of spanking rather than a biblical form of chastisement. They had used the rod without the reproof. They had punished the wrong without explaining the right and most often they had punished in anger and with a wrong motive. Any time parents reject God's methods and embrace worldly methods, problems will result. Proverbs 14:12 tells us, "There is a way that seems right to a man, but in the end it leads to destruction." In these cases it would have been better for the parents to refrain from spanking altogether than to administer spanking in a way that rejected God's holy intention for discipline.

The use of the rod according to godly principles is clearly taught in the scriptures, as we shall see in the next sections. To say, "I don't believe in spanking," is to say that God's ordained methods for child training are wrong. It's to reject God's Word. It's to say that you are wiser than God Himself. God's ways are higher than our ways. "'For my thoughts are not your thoughts, neither are your ways my ways,' declares the Lord. 'As the heavens are higher than the earth, so are my ways higher than your ways and my thoughts than your thoughts.'" (Isa. 55:8–9)

What Exactly is the Rod?

Tedd Tripp defines using the rod as "A parent, in faith toward God and faithfulness toward his or her children, undertaking the responsibility of careful, timely, measured and controlled use of physical punishment to underscore the importance of obeying God, thus rescuing the child from continuing in his foolishness until death."[1]

Why is Spanking Necessary?

Spanking is part of God's ordained method for driving the foolishness out of the hearts of our children. We are told in Proverbs 22:15: "Folly is bound up in the heart of a child but the rod of discipline will drive it far from him." This verse also clearly defines what our motive should be in spanking our children. It's not to get revenge for embarrassing or irritating us or to get them to just outwardly comply, but to drive out the foolishness that is bound up in their hearts. And as I mentioned in part one, if you can reach their hearts, the behavior will take care of itself.

Worldly Methods Used by Parents in an Attempt to Obtain Obedience

In an effort to avoid a biblical use of the rod for discipline, some parents have come up with shallow and destructive methods to obtain obedience.

Worldly Method #1: Bribing

I once observed a mom in Wal-Mart telling her two-year-old to come to her. The child ignored her mom and took off running the other way. In desperation Mom called out, "Come to Mommy and I'll give you a sucker." Immediately the child went from hearing impaired to exceptional hearing and came quickly to Mom's side. This is not training for obedience; it's rewarding the child for stubbornness. Children should be taught to obey because it is right and because it pleases God, not to get a reward. Giving them a reward in order to get them to obey encourages them in selfishness. Their motive for obeying is, "I'll obey for what I can get out of it."

Worldly Method #2: Threatening

This one usually comes after you have repeated your instructions several times to no avail and so you pull out the "big guns."

101

"If you don't start sharing your toys right now I'm going to send them all off to kids who will share!" the threatening parent says. This teaches them that Mommy doesn't mean what she says. How many of your parents, in an attempt to persuade you to appreciate your toys, talked about the kids on the other side of the world who didn't have any toys? But how many of your parents actually packed up all of your toys and shipped them off to Timbuktu?

Avoid saying things that you don't mean. Recently I caught myself threatening my children. I said, "If you don't get your room clean, you are not spending the night with Nana and Papa tonight." But I knew good and well that I wasn't about to forfeit my date night with my husband in order to follow through with this threat! Matthew 5:37 says, "Simply let your 'Yes' be 'Yes,' and your 'No' be 'No'; anything beyond this comes from the evil one." We are to say what we mean and mean what we say or we can exasperate our children. It's hard to take a liar seriously. Never, never, issue a warning or a command without following it through. Think before you speak. Try not to say "yes" or "no" to something until you are sure that it is your definite answer. James 1:19 tells us to be "quick to listen and slow to speak." Proverbs 15:28 tells us that "The heart of the righteous weighs its answers."

Worldly Method #3: Appealing to their emotions

Parents often try to appeal to the emotions of the child by making them feel guilty. "After all I do for you, this is how you repay me," moans the parent with a sad face. This worldly method can be especially tempting to parents who are stretched thin already, much of it in service to their children. It's easy to feel sorry for ourselves and think that our children "owe us" obedience. However, this teaches children to be man-pleasers rather than God-pleasers. John 12:43 teaches us to love praise from God and not from man. We want our children's motives for obeying to come from a heart to please God not from a parent inflicted guilt trip.

Worldly Method # 4: Manipulating their environment

While Mom is talking to a friend, little Rusty grabs a vase off the end table. Mom looks over her shoulder and continues talking to her friend while she puts the vase high up on the shelf where Rusty can't reach it. Well, little rambunctious Rusty (he's just curious, you know) now grabs the crystal frame from the other end table. After he has smudged his chocolate-stained fingerprints all over it, Mom eventually notices that he has it. "Rusty, put that back," snaps Mom. Rusty puts it back, waits a minute, then grabs it again. So Mom gets up and places the crystal frame high on the shelf where Rusty can't reach it. And history repeats itself until Mom has succeeded in rearranging the whole living room while little Rusty (he's so cute) looks for something that Mom can't move. Notice that Mom has trained Rusty. The principle she has trained him in is this: "If you can reach it, it's yours. If I put it where only I can reach it, it's mine." But she has failed to teach Rusty about self-control and obedience.

Worldly Method # 5: Reasoning with the child

Mom asks her six-year-old, "Honey, don't you want to come and eat lunch now?" "No, thanks, Mom, I'm playing with my cars."

"Oh, but Sweetie, your hot dog will get cold if you don't come now."

"Well, I'd rather come when I'm done playing."

103

"But if you'll come on now and eat, I thought we could
go to the park after lunch."
"Okay, Mom, I'll be there in a minute."

Here Mom is attempting to talk her son into obedience,
rather than simply instructing him and expecting him to obey.
Parents who try to reason with their child normally end up
frustrated and quite often outwitted. And they usually wind
up resorting to a bribe in order to get the response they're
after. Reasoning with small children in an attempt to get them
to obey causes confusion because it places them in a position
that they are not mature or responsible enough to handle. It
erases the line of authority between the adult and the child
and places the child on a peer level with the parent. Instead,
clearly instruct your child and expect obedience.

Worldly methods such as these are just a few ways to
manipulate a child's behavior, but they all fail to reach the
heart. Colossians 2:8 tells us, "See to it that no one takes
you captive through hollow and deceptive philosophy, which
depends on human tradition and the basic principles of this
world rather than on Christ." And Galatians 6:7–8 says,
"Do not be deceived: God cannot be mocked. A man reaps
what he sows. The one who sows to please his sinful nature,
from that nature will reap destruction; the one who sows to
please the Spirit, from the Spirit will reap eternal life."

We live in an age that defies God and His Word at every
point, including child training. But the Bible says, "There is
a way that seems right to man, but in the end it leads to
death." (Prov. 14:1) We shouldn't be surprised that worldly
methods and false philosophies are taught by secular
"experts." However, we must learn to discern the difference
between the wisdom of the world and the wisdom of God.
1 Corinthians 3:18 says, "The wisdom of this world is foolishness in God's sight."

I'd like to give you two common scenarios where Mom left out using God's Word in training her children and I'd like you to notice how both scenarios end.

Scenario #1: A mother waits in the check-out line at the grocery store with her four-year-old son. As little Tommy begins rummaging through the candy stand, Mom grabs his arm and says, "Tommy, I told you to stand right here!"

Tommy jerks free of Mom's grasp. "I don't want to," he says defiantly, and returns to the candy.

Mom's voice goes up an octave. "Tommy, you get back over here right now or you're going to get it when we get home!" The battle continues as the clerk rings up, bags, and places the groceries in the buggy. Mother and son ride home from the grocery store frustrated and angry.

Scenario #2: A mother waits in line at the main counter in the public library with her two preschool-age children. The children begin to argue and push one another until Mom says, "Stop it right now! You know that is not how you are supposed to act!" As the librarian stamps the small stack of books, Mom begins to explain, "I'm sorry for the disturbance; they haven't had their nap yet." On the way out Mom tells the children how disappointed she is in their behavior.

Notice how both of these scenarios ended on a negative note. It's because Mom is not heeding God's commands in training her children. She has abandoned God's Holy instructions and adopted worldly methods.

When training is done properly, it should always end on a positive note. A child who directly disobeys mom in the grocery store should not be yelled at or have to ride home with an angry mom. This sort of discipline does not show unconditional love and careful instruction. It sends the negative message, "I am not pleased with you" for the child to ponder. Our desire should be for the child to ponder what he could have done right rather than what he did wrong.

The mom who takes the time to properly spank the child while assuring him of her love, and then discusses with the child what he could have done instead, sends the positive message, "I love you enough to train you in what is right."

It's the same in the second scenario. The children first witnessed the mom offer excuses for their behavior, which sends the negative message, "It's okay to argue and push one another if you are tired." Then she sends the children mixed signals by contradicting herself when she stated that she is disappointed in their behavior. Again, this causes the children to ponder their mom's disapproval rather than a positive character quality. The mom's training would have been more effective and heart-oriented if she would have calmly told the children to fold their hands and wait quietly for her to check out. If they chose to disobey her instructions, on the way out she could have explained that she loves them so much that she must teach them self-control and obedience. After administering discipline at home, she could have discussed what a positive response to her instructions in the library would have been. This sends the positive message, "I love you enough to train you in self-control and obedience so that you will make wiser decisions."

10

The Biblical Model Works

H ave you ever heard of a parent who did not want their children to obey? Of course you haven't. All parents desire obedient children, yet many parents fail to get obedience. Some become so discouraged and frustrated they convince themselves that obedience is not even possible with their children.

Why are parents discouraged to the point of giving up? Why isn't discipline working with their children? Why are their children spiraling down into the depths of disobedience? Why do many parents often resort to screaming, pleading, threatening, and even physical abuse in their attempt to train their children—all to no avail? It's because they are not following the instructions in the "instruction manual,"[1] the Bible. Roy Lessin says:

When someone buys a new appliance he is provided with an instruction manual by the manufacturer. It tells how to use the appliance and how to keep it in the best working order. If something goes wrong the customer is encouraged to contact the manufacturer for repairs. So it is with family. The family is God's idea. He brought it into being. In His Word He has given clear instructions as to how He intends it to function. When parents experience problems in training their children, He is the one to be consulted. He has given parents the rich counsel of His wisdom to guide them in the important matter of training their children.[2]

Why Do We Use the Rod?

Biblical discipline involves teaching, rebuking, correcting and the proper use of the rod. You might be thinking, "Why would a loving parent ever spank their child?"

The use of the rod demonstrates faithfulness to God. Parents who place their confidence in the wisdom of God understand the relationship between the rod and obedience. To heed God's commands in using the rod is to fully rely upon His wisdom and to faithfully trust in His counsel.

The use of the rod demonstrates faithfulness toward the child. Parents who refuse to spank are doing their children a spiritual injustice. Not to spank is to be unfaithful to the soul of the child. "Do not withhold discipline from a child; if you punish him with the rod, he will not die. Punish him with the rod and save his soul from death." (Prov. 23:13–14) This does not mean that the more you spank the more likely it is that your child will go to heaven. It simply means that the use of the rod helps to bring the child to compliance and to a point where he is more likely to receive the Word of God.

The use of the rod imparts wisdom. The connection of the rod with wisdom throughout the Scriptures is very important. The child who is not submitting to parental authority is acting foolishly. He is rejecting the jurisdiction of God. The rod of correction brings wisdom to the child. It humbles the heart of the child and drives out the foolishness that is bound up there. The Bible explains it this way: "The rod of correction imparts wisdom, but a child left to himself disgraces his mother." (Prov. 29:15)

The Rod is a Responsibility

When parents administer the rod they are not merely punishing their children. They are obeying the responsibility that God has given them. The rod is somewhat of a mystery in how it works but we can be confident that while we are obeying God and working on the buttocks, God is honoring our obedience and working on the heart. Therefore, if you are going to rescue your child from death, if you are going to uproot and drive the foolishness out of his heart, and if you are going to impart wisdom, you must use the rod.

Excuses Parents Use for Not Spanking Their Children

Parents of more recent generations have come up with lots of excuses for not spanking their children. Although many of these excuses are well-meaning, they are not biblical.

"But . . . I love my children so much that I am unable to spank them." I can certainly relate to that way of thinking. One of the hardest things I do as a mother is administering the rod. Spanking my children is painful for me. I never believed my parents when they spoke those famous parental words, "This is going to hurt me more than it hurts you." I always thought to myself, "Bologna." However, now that the tables have turned, I know that my parents spoke the truth. To purposely inflict pain on your child is a hard thing

to do. But it is worldly thinking that says, "I just love him too much to spank him."

Ask yourself this question: Who benefits from your decision to not spank your child? Certainly not the child. Proverbs 23 makes it clear that failure to discipline with the rod places the child at risk. So who benefits from not using the rod? You do. You are delivered from the discomfort of spanking your child. You are delivered from inflicting pain on one who is so precious to you. You are delivered from the inconvenience of taking the time to discipline the right way. But God says, "He who spares the rod hates his son, but he who loves him is careful to discipline him." (Prov. 13:24) Parents are not to be abusive, but *careful* to discipline. So it is love that motivates a parent to use the rod. God associates discipline with love so when we discipline in love, *our children* will associate discipline with love.

"But . . . he's not old enough to understand."[3] Some parents entertain the idea that Junior is just too young to understand that he isn't allowed to pull everything off the end tables. Children are old enough to learn "No" when they are old enough to do something that requires you to tell them "No." I've heard moms brag about how smart their babies are; their six-month-old can wave bye-bye or clap his hands and play pat-a-cake upon encouragement. By eight months he has an enormous understanding of vocabulary. He responds to instructions such as, "Come to Mama," "Blow kisses," and "Hug your baby doll." Yet these same moms who brag about how smart their babies are say, "Oh, he's just too young to understand the word 'No.'"

I've had moms ask me when is it okay to slap their baby's hand for disobeying and touching something that is off limits. The answer should be obvious. When they disobey and touch something that is off limits. If they are old enough to disobey then they are old enough to be trained to obey.

My friend, Debra, recounted the struggle she had with getting her baby to stay seated in the high chair. The baby was ten months old when she learned to obey. Mom decided that if she was old enough to demonstrate defiance, she was old enough to learn compliance. Mom reflects back on the day Della learned to obey in this area:

> She pushed herself to a half-stand in the seat; I said, "No, Della, don't stand in your chair," and sat her down. She promptly sprang back up so I popped her diapered behind and said, "No! Sit down." She looked confused, eased down, then back up, watching me, thought better of it, sat back down, and never gave us another problem about standing in her high chair.

Della learned her lesson the first time Mom disciplined her. Not all children come to a point of compliance this quickly, but this example certainly proves that a ten-month-old is capable of learning the meaning of the word "No."

"But . . . he's only acting this way because we're not at home."[4] Your child's disobedience comes from his heart, not from a change in surroundings. When you are away from home, you must not blame your child's disobedience on the new setting. If his behavior is excused because he is away from home, he will quickly learn that he is only required to obey at home. It's a double standard that will not benefit the child, the parent, or those involved in his outings. Your word should be obeyed at the grocery store, at the park, at the mall, at a friend's house, and EVEN at Grandma's house.

"But . . . I don't think he feels well because he only acts like this when he's sick."[5] If your child is sick he needs Mom's special care. He needs lots of love, rest, and possibly medicine. However, disobedience must not be excused because the child is "not feeling well." There is nothing in the Scriptures to validate the neglect of training because the child is tired or

sick. The Bible does not say that children should be trained to obey *except* when they are sick. God's Word is always the same. If your child has a fever, a runny nose, or a tummy ache, "Yes" still means "Yes" and " No" still means "No." Parents who neglect training their children every time the child has the sniffles find themselves with the difficult task of retraining later. It's always easier to train than to retrain.

But . . . he gets it from his Uncle Tom. He has a bad temper, too."[6] It may be too late to correct Uncle Tom's temper with the rod, (although I do think there are many adults who could benefit from a good old fashioned "whuppin," as we say in Alabama) but it's not too late for your child. The fact that Uncle Tom was not trained in self-control should serve as a motivator, not an excuse. To blame sin on the child's heritage is to state the obvious. *In one sense, all* sin is hereditary. We inherited it from Adam. But rest assured, the biblical use of the rod helps to deal with any hereditary trait that needs correcting.

"But . . . spanking doesn't work with my child." A mother once said to me, "You may be able to get your kids to obey, but it won't work with my kids." She went on to explain how different her children's personalities were. Each child is a unique creation of God, but he expects all children to obey regardless of their personality. Each child has distinctive physical features, personalities, and abilities, but nowhere in the Scripture does it state that any child is an exception to God's command for obedience. Colossians 3:20 says, "Children, obey your parents in everything, for this pleases the Lord."

Reasons that Spanking Does Not Work

In some cases, spanking does not have the desired effect of training the child's heart. Usually this can be attributed to improper application of the rod, of which there are several varieties:

Lack of Consistency. You have to be consistent. Bruce Ray says, "It is not the severity of correction which will produce obedience; it is the certainty of correction which will bring about the desired result. Be consistent in your administration of discipline. Never, never, never issue a warning or a command without following it through." [7]

One day Johnny's mom ignores him as he drags all the Tupperware out of the kitchen cabinet. But the next day he gets a spanking for it. How confusing, exasperating, and unfair this is to the child! If he never knows when you might strike, he'll spend his childhood walking on eggshells. We have to set the standard and be consistent in following through with consequences when that standard is violated, or we can exasperate our children and provoke them to anger.

A child who never knows what to expect can also become insecure. There is a great sense of security in knowing what to expect. What's cruel is for them to live in fear because they don't know what might happen next. What's cruel is for their discipline to be based on the mood, energy level, or whim of the parent. All children, whether infants, toddlers, or youths find much security in knowing where their boundaries are. Really, with boundaries comes freedom. When you establish boundaries for your children you are giving them the freedom to determine when there will be consequences. They are corrected by their own choice rather than the emotion or mood of the parent. A secure child is a child that knows his boundaries and is consistently corrected when he oversteps them.

The rod of correction returns the child to a place of submission to his parents, a place where God has promised blessing. Discipline enables him to gain self-control. Discipline helps him to respect Mom and Dad and promotes an atmosphere of closeness between the parent and the child. The mom who is consistent and does not allow the child to challenge her authority will experience intimacy with her child. But when he is allowed to be sullen and disobedient, distance can develop. Don't be deceived into thinking that spanking will hinder closeness. The parent who is consistent in requiring obedience keeps the relationship in balance. This parent will enjoy a close and open relationship with the child.

Lack of Persistence. Some parents give the rod a couple of days, become discouraged when their children are not transformed overnight, and they give up. They decide that discipline is not only unpleasant; but it doesn't work either. In Hebrews 12:11 we read that, "No discipline seems pleasant at the time but painful. Later on, however, it produces a harvest of righteousness and peace for those who have been trained by it" (Emphasis added). You reap what you sow, you reap later than you sow, and you reap more than you sow.

When we are persistent, our children learn the law of the harvest. Tedd Tripp says, "When disobedience is met with painful consequences they learn that God has built the principle of sowing and reaping into their world."[8] We may become discouraged at times and think that it's no use, but our responsibility is to trust God and do what He says and then leave the results to Him. Proverbs 3:5 says to "Trust in the Lord with all your heart and lean not on your on understanding." God wants us to do all that he requires for as long as it takes. He challenges us in Galatians 6:9, "Let us not become weary in doing good, for at the proper time we will reap a harvest if we do not give up."

Lack of Effectiveness. The purpose of a spanking is to inflict pain. If little Johnny is sporting an extra padded diaper and running in circles while Mom half-heartedly administers the rod, the spanking is ineffective. (See chapter 12 for "Guidelines for Administering Biblical Chastisement.") Keep in mind that every child is different. Some have a higher tolerance for pain than others. Some are naturally more compliant than others and are quicker to demonstrate sincere repentance. As a mother, you have to determine what is "effective" with your child. Please note that if you ever leave a bruise on your child, you are spanking too hard.

Lack of Righteousness. When the rod is administered in sinful anger or with a wrong motive, the child will resent rather than repent. Children will not yield to correction when it is administered in unrighteous anger or if the parent disciplines for selfish reasons. And God will not honor our efforts if they are conducted in sin. It's okay for the child to wait in his room for Mom to pray a few minutes and get her heart right before administering the rod. Make sure your motive for disciplining your children is righteous and not out of anger because James 1:20 tells us that "Man's anger does not bring about the righteous life that God desires." Your motive should not be revenge but love. It should be to drive out the foolishness from the child's heart. Discipline shouldn't be an "I'll show you!" mentality, or a "Boy, you're gonna get it now!" It should be, "I love you too much to allow this sin to take root in your heart and grow."

11

Setting the Standard of Obedience

W e should expect instant obedience from our children. Teach them that God wants them to obey "all the way, right away, and with a happy heart." As soon as my children could talk, I would ask them, "How does God want you to obey?" They would respond, "All the way, right away, and with a happy heart." I've talked a lot about training children with this standard, so allow me to break down each point and back up each with Scripture.

Obedience Should Be All the Way. The Bible states that obedience must be complete. God demonstrates the importance of complete obedience through the life of King Saul in 1 Samuel 15. God told Saul to completely destroy the Amalekites, including all of their livestock. Saul got to thinking about what a waste it would be to kill all the livestock, so he took it upon himself to keep a few. After the battle, Samuel questioned King Saul by asking if he had fully obeyed God's command. I'm sure the blood went to Saul's face as he nodded his head. Then Saul's heart probably skipped a beat as the sheep began to bleat in the background. Saul was caught with his hand in the cookie jar, and just like a child who says, "I was only getting one for you, Mom," Saul tried to justify his disobedience by stating that he was only saving them to offer as sacrifices to God. But Samuel replied, "To obey is better than sacrifice." As a consequence of King Saul's lack of complete obedience, the kingdom was taken from him.[1]

Obedience Should Be Right Away. Any time my pastor preaches on obedience, he always ends with the classic injunction, "Delayed obedience is disobedience." A child should be trained to respond promptly the first time the parent gives a command. The parent should not have to yell, threaten, or repeat instructions in order to achieve obedience. The command that should be obeyed is to be spoken in a normal tone of voice and only one time. The consequences of delayed obedience are seen in the life of Jonah. God told Jonah to go to Nineveh. In the end Jonah did go. But the consequences of his delayed obedience put his life and the life of many others in great spiritual and physical danger. Instant obedience should be the standard, and children should be expected to abide by that standard. We should reinforce that expectation with the rod each and every time they fail to obey—or we'll be sending them mixed signals.[2]

Obedience Should Be With a Joyful Heart. God requires not only *outward* obedience but also *inward* obedience. Inward obedience comes from a heart that is joyful. If a child is obeying with a wrong attitude, he is not obeying in a way that pleases God. A child who obeys outwardly but is inwardly angry because he didn't get his own way is a child who is not truly happy. True happiness permeates the child who delights in obeying because he knows that he is pleasing both God and his parents. Happiness and contentment are heart choices. Children can choose to obey with a happy heart. Parents must guide them in doing so.

When Wesley was younger, I can say with certainty that he had more spankings for disobeying *with his attitude* than for *direct disobedience*. He would do what I told him but he would stomp and pout in the process. It took a lot of correction to teach him that complete obedience is expressed with a joyful heart and a right attitude.

Right attitudes are not issues of the emotions. They are issues of the will, which means that a child can choose to be happy and content. And God has called him to do this in Philippians 2:14: "Do everything without complaining or arguing." And 1 Thessalonians 5:16–18 says, "Be joyful always; pray continually; give thanks in all circumstances, for this is God's will for you in Christ Jesus." Roy Lessin says,

> The feelings or emotions are a barometer of the will. When a child chooses the proper attitude, the appropriate emotional response will follow.[3]

Even a small child can be told, "Sweetie, you need to obey Mama with a happy heart." I still have to remind Wesley that his attitude is a choice. Emotions are good, but I don't want for him to be a slave to his emotions—so I remind him, "Honey, you are choosing to have a bad attitude, where you should be choosing to obey with a right attitude."

Now, children should be allowed to come and freely talk about their thoughts and feelings and ask questions, but this should be done in a pleasant tone of voice and with an attitude of respect. In other words, a child with a disrespectful attitude might say, "Why do you have to give me a ridiculous bedtime of 8:00?" A child who wants to address this issue respectfully might ask, "Now that I am nine years old, could we discuss my bedtime?"

Avoiding Traps

To elicit your child's prompt obedience with a willing heart, you must avoid these traps that will sabotage your efforts at proper training.

Repeating Yourself. There are some parents who will tell their children two or three times to do something before they will do it. If we are in the habit of not requiring instant obedience, then we are causing our children to be in the habit of not obeying instantly.

Raising Your Voice. Other parents have to raise their voice beyond the normal range before their children will obey. They issue the first command and the child thinks, "Oh, I've got plenty of time." Then the command comes at them a little louder and the child looks up to examine the parent and thinks, "Oh, still got some time, her eyeballs and neck veins aren't bulging yet." Then finally, when Mom has turned green, swelled to bursting out of her clothes, and transformed into the "Hulk," they obey.

Worldly Techniques. Then there are those parents who say, "If you don't do this by the time I count to three, you're going to get it, Mister!" They count: "One" . . . the child doesn't move; "Two" . . . the child still doesn't move; "Two and a half" . . . and so it goes. Children will rise to the standard that the parents set. If you don't expect your child to obey until the count of three, then he will not obey until you count. Why not expect instant obedience? This standard leaves no room for question or confusion. It's much easier and much more peaceful. If my child is stepping off the curb into a busy street, I don't want to have to count to three in order for him to obey.

Most importantly, we are training them and preparing them to obey Jesus. Parents are often responsible for the habits of their children. We want them to be in the habit of obeying us the first time so that when they surrender to the Lordship of Christ they will find it easier to obey Him the first time. So before you begin your count to three, ask yourself, "Do I want my child to be in the habit of obeying God the first time, the second time, or the third time?"

Training children to quickly obey ought to be the standard. We need to be aware of things like repeating instructions two or three times, raising our voices, or giving them till the count of three. These things draw us away from training our children to instantly and completely obey.

Tolerating Small Acts of Disobedience. We also need to be aware of only correcting major acts of disobedience while letting minor acts slide. About 100 years ago, J.C Ryle warned parents, "Beware of letting small faults pass unnoticed under the idea it is a little one. There are no little things in training children; all are important. Little weeds need plucking up as much as any. Leave them alone and they will soon be great."[4] Anyone with a garden knows the importance of being consistent with little weeds. If they are let go all summer they are incredibly hard to pull. It was easy when the roots were small and didn't go very deep. But to pluck out those weeds later is a backbreaking job because they have been overlooked for so long. The roots have gone deeply and spread widely.

I can tell you through personal experience that it is the same with children. Once again, it's much easier to train than to retrain. Often I have found myself in a rut. My children will do great for weeks and then little acts of disobedience or disrespect start creeping in and I let them go because they have been doing so well. The next thing I know, I'm frustrated, I'm repeating myself, and I'm raising my voice. It's my fault. It's because I have not been obedient to God in training them consistently and diligently in righteousness. And because of my disobedience and neglect, my relationship with my children is not as intimate and open. Tension and frustration have crept into our relationship and robbed us of the openness and closeness that we usually share. We all suffer the consequences of my disobedience.

It's at these times that I have to sit them down and say, "Kids, I need to ask your forgiveness. Mama has been allowing you to disobey. I have not been training you the way that I should. It is my responsibility to train you in wisdom but I have been allowing you to behave foolishly."

I also explain to them that I have asked my heavenly Father to forgive me for my disobedience. Not only is this a critical step for me but it also models biblical confession and repentance for them. It is beneficial to allow the child to actually listen in on the prayer. My next step is to go over what is expected (we go over the standard) and I tell them that I love them too much to allow them to disobey and live foolishly.

Waiting Until the Teapot Boils. The tendency to overlook disobedience is often based on the mood or emotion of the parent. Some of us have what Bruce Ray calls a "teapot temper."

A teapot temper is characterized by outward calm but inward turmoil. Outwardly everything seems fine, but inwardly a lot of little things are beginning to agitate and boil until finally a lot of noise escapes from the little hole in the top of the kettle. Suddenly, we blow up and grab little Jimmy. We throw him across our knee and then really let him have it, giving him a spanking like he has never had before in his life. Somehow, we think that that one spanking is going to

make up for all the little things that Jimmy has done throughout the day.[5]

This sort of discipline is wrong because it's based on mood
and emotion. The spanking was a release of Mom's frustration, not a self-controlled act of love. A good spanking
at the end of the day can never make up for the spankings
that should have been administered throughout the day.
Moms who have a teapot temper need to depend on God's
grace to enable them to act contrary to their nature and in
harmony with the Word of God.

12

To Spank or Not To Spank

I n spite of what I've said about the importance of spanking, I also believe there are occasions that may appear to be discipline situations, but do not justify spanking. It is inappropriate to spank for the following reasons:

Childish Behavior. Children are naturally immature and should not be disciplined for acting in accordance with their age. There is a difference between *childishness* and *foolishness*. Childishness becomes foolishness when the child has been given clear instructions and understands those instructions but chooses to disobey.

For example, it's childishness for Sally May to play slip-slide in the tub and get the floor all wet. Sally May should not be disciplined for a childish act such as this. But this same behavior becomes foolishness if Mom clearly instructed her to not play slip-slide and she does it anyway and gets the floor all wet. Then she should be disciplined for being foolish.

Inability to Perform. Parents must guard against using a spanking for trying to force a child to perform athletically or intellectually. When I say intellectually, I'm talking about spanking a child because he made a "C" in school even though he puts forth the effort of studying. All children have their own God-given talents and abilities. Some may love to read while others love to draw. Some may love to play sports while others love to play a musical instrument. Parents should not try to change the natural abilities and the personal desires (or interests) of their children.

Accidents. Unintentional accidents, like spilling drinks, are also not reasons to spank. Accidents can be frustrating for Mom but ask yourself, "Did the accident occur as a result of the child being disobedient?"

If Tommy accidentally spills his cup of red Kool-Aid on the new carpet in the living room, that is not an act of disobedience and he should not be disciplined for it (though it would be appropriate to have the child help clean up). However, if Mom clearly instructed Tommy to drink his Kool-Aid in the kitchen and to not travel into the living room with it, but he spills it on the carpet, chastisement would be in order. This would not be because he accidentally spilled it, but because he willfully disobeyed your command to stay in the kitchen with his drink.

Before Having All of the Facts. Another time when a spanking should not be given is when you do not have all the facts surrounding the circumstances. There have been many times that I have had to apologize for jumping to conclusions before I had all the facts straight.

We have a creek behind our house that has a little bridge you can cross over to get into the woods. My kids love to cross over that bridge and play in the woods. However, one

126

day they decided that the creek looked more intriguing than the woods so they indulged themselves in creek activities which involved getting wet and muddy. They seemed to enjoy it so much that I played the "cool" mommy and enthusiastically listened to the great adventures they had enjoyed in the creek. Well, naturally the newfound play area lured them back the next day . . . and the next day . . . and the next day, until finally, I was willing to forfeit being "cool" for a break from wet, muddy clothes and children.

I laid down the law. "Kids, the creek has been great, but it's time to stop getting muddy and wet every day. You may not play in the creek any more. You may cross over the bridge and play in the woods but no more creek. Everyone clear?" Two little heads nodded an affirmative reply.

It wasn't but two days later when here comes Wesley into the garage, pants soaking wet and mud squishing up from between his toes. He opened his mouth to speak but before he said one word, I lit right in. I immediately started rattling off about how he had disobeyed me. I informed him that he would lose the privilege of playing outside for a week.

When I finally closed my yap trap, I looked down. There was a look of total exasperation on both of their little faces. Through tears and a quivering lip, Wesley began to explain how they were crossing over the bridge to play in the woods when Alex accidentally dropped her teddy bear into the creek. He went on to tell about how upset she became. She was fearfully crying out, "He's gonna drown, Wesley! He's gonna drown!"

Then, as he wrapped his arms around my leg, he concluded, "Mama, I knew you told us not to go in the creek but I tried to think of what you would want me to do. Alex was so upset and I just thought you would want me to get her teddy bear for her."

Ouch, ouch, and ouch. I was wrong, and I had to ask them to forgive me for jumping to conclusions before I had all of the facts straight. The Bible warns us, "He who answers before listening—that is his folly and his shame." (Prov. 18:13)

While You Are Angry. As I have already stated, a parent who spanks a child in anger is sinning against God and sinning against their child. If you are angry, take time to pray through your anger and allow God to make your motives pure before you spank. Disciplining in anger can cause the child to resent rather than repent.

When is the Rod Necessary?

We know from Proverbs 22:15 that foolishness is bound up in the heart of the child and we know that it is the rod of discipline that drives out that foolishness. Biblically, we discipline for foolishness. So what exactly is foolishness? Roy Lessin says, "This word refers a selfish disposition of the heart that disregards God's wisdom and will, choosing to live independently of Him." [1]

The rod is useful for correcting these areas of foolishness:

1. *Direct Disobedience.* Direct disobedience is when you have given your child clear instructions and made sure he understood those instructions, but he chooses to disobey. "Children obey your parents in everything for this pleases the Lord." (Col. 3:20)

2. *Defiant Attitude.* A defiant attitude is when the child expresses rebellion in his actions, words, tone of voice, or facial expressions. "Serve the Lord with gladness." (Psa. 100:2) "Do everything without complaining or arguing." (Phil. 2:14)

128

Guidelines for Administering Biblical Chastisement

Administering the rod without following biblical principles can be counter-productive and even dangerous or harmful to the child. Always follow these guidelines when spanking your child. The following guidelines are for you and your child; you would only spank another person's child if you had his or her permission.

Discuss what the child has done wrong and why it is your responsibility to spank him. You might probe his heart by asking him questions like, "Was God pleased with what you did? What was wrong with what you did?" Make sure he knows that you spank him because you love him too much to allow the sin to take root in his heart and grow. Remember to use biblical terminology when reproving your child because, according to Hebrews 4:12, it is God's Word that will truly penetrate the child's heart. It is also important for the child to verbally confess what he has done and ask for forgiveness.

Guide the child in thinking through what he should have done. Ask him, "What *could you* have done in this situation that would have been better?" Let him think through it. That's teaching him how to "think" like a Christian.

Use the proper instrument as your spanker. You do not want to use something so stiff that you bruise your child. Use something with a little flex so that it stings without bruising.

Let the child know how many swats you will be administering. Telling your child how many "swats" he will receive demonstrates that you are using self-control. If the child does not come to a point of repentance and

129

compliance, it may be necessary to administer another spanking.

Spank as promptly after the offense as possible. Take the child's age into account. Promptness is even more important with younger children. A two-year-old who disobeys while company is over for dinner should not be spanked two hours later, after the company leaves. Although it may be an inconvenient time, justice for the child would be to politely excuse yourself and the child for a time of correction. However, a four-year-old who disobeys while in the grocery store can certainly wait until the groceries are purchased and carried home to receive chastisement.

Administer the spanking in private. Remember that your goal is not to embarrass or humiliate your child but to bring him to repentance. A repentant heart will not result from a child whose primary focus is on being embarrassed in front of friends or siblings (or the audience in the check-out line).

Administer the rod to the child's bottom. The bottom is a sensitive area yet it is cushioned in such a way that a proper spanking will not do physical damage.

Take time for reconciliation. This requires Mom's forgiveness. When our children sin we are not to hold a grudge. Mark Twain once said, "Forgiveness is the fragrance the violet sheds on the heel that crushed it." I once spoke to a mom's group on the issue of spanking. During the Q&A session a mom stated, "My child wants me to hug him right after he receives a spanking. I am unable to oblige him because I am so mad. I just need time to 'cool off' a while before I can 'make up' with him." This mom should have never spanked the child to begin with if she was this angry. We are commanded to forgive just as Jesus forgave—and to forgive without delay.

No matter what they have done or how badly they have embarrassed or hurt us, it is *nothing* compared to what we did to the spotless Lamb of God. It was because of our sins against him that he suffered and died on the cross at Calvary. And in the heat of the moment, while he hung there, suffering in agonizing and unbearable physical and spiritual pain, his love and forgiveness were evident in his words, "Father, forgive them." Holding a grudge is sinful. Jesus didn't take time to "cool off." His forgiveness was instant and complete. We have no right to withhold forgiveness from our children even in the heat of the moment. Colossians 3:13 says, "Forgive as the Lord forgave you." What a holy example of sacrificial, unconditional, true love Jesus set for us that day at Calvary.

Require the child to make restitution. In most cases with small children this is simply a matter of having the child go back and practice what is right. In some cases restitution might entail more. Perhaps the child stole a piece of candy; restitution would be in asking for forgiveness *and* paying back the owner of the candy. Restitution is more than just asking for forgiveness: it's going back and making things right. And it's a very important part of training them in righteousness.

After the spanking is over, take the child into your arms and tell him how much you love him. His slate is clean. He was disobedient and he has been properly disciplined, so put the issue to rest.

In Conclusion

We often question our methods and wonder if we are raising our children correctly. If we make sure that the methods we use for disciplining, training, and instructing our children originate from Scripture, we can be confident that we are raising our children the right way, which is God's way.

Perhaps you have not been training your children in accordance with God's Word and after reading this book you fear that it is too late. Take heart, dear friend! It is never too late! I can testify to that! You see, I was not brought up in a Christian home. Although my parents were extremely moral people, my family never even stepped foot inside a church until I was seventeen years old. My parents were basically through raising my brother and me when they accepted Jesus Christ as their Lord and Savior. As they learned about God's plan for the family in the Bible, their hearts broke because Jesus had been left out of our lives for so many years. But they were encouraged not to give up on their rebellious children. They prayed and sought God's Word for how to make up for all those years of leaving Him out of our family. They drew strength from the many promises of God. One verse in particular that stood out to them was Joel 2:25a: "I will repay you for the years the locusts have eaten."

My Daddy knelt beside my bed late one night, took my hands in his, and asked me to forgive him for not raising me in the ways of the Lord. From that moment on, my parents were diligent in pursuing God's will for our family. As a result of their passion to please God, in word and action, I accepted Jesus as my Lord and Savior when I was eighteen years old. God is faithful, and His Word never returns void (see Isa. 55:11).

I would like to encourage you to keep searching and learning from your holy instruction manual, the Bible. What a blessing it is that God has not left us to figure out how to raise our children on our own. He has provided us with everything we need for life and godliness. Please know that this book does not contain everything that you need to know for raising your children. You can't do step A and then step

B and always get C as a result. If you depend only on the information I have provided, you will wind up defeated and confused. You must be 100% dependent upon God and His Word. His will is not for us to be defeated and confused, but dependent upon Him. And when we acknowledge Him in all our ways, He promises to give us wisdom and make our paths straight. "Trust in the Lord with all your heart and lean not on your own understanding; in all your ways acknowledge him, and he will make your paths straight" (Prov. 3:5–6).

Training our children in righteousness is a process, but God promises that just like laboring in a garden, we will reap what we sow. Let us keep on sowing the seeds of righteousness. I can think of no better garden to plant those seeds in than in the soil of my children's hearts. To God be the Glory.

How to Become a Christian

W hen asked, "Are you a Christian?" most Americans will say, "Yes." According to statistics, most Americans believe in God and think they will go to Heaven when they die. However, the Bible says, "Enter through the narrow gate. For wide is the gate and broad is the road that leads to destruction, and many enter through it. But small is the gate and narrow the road that leads to life, and only a few find it." (Matt. 7:13–14) Why do so many people think that they are Christians if they are not? A false Christian is deceived by what seems logical to him. "There is a way that seems right to a man, but in the end it leads to death." (Prov. 14:12)

A False Christian

Believes in God—Simply believing in God does not make you a Christian. Satan himself, along with all the demons of Hell, believes in God. James says, "You believe that there is one God. Good! Even the demons believe that – and shudder." (James 2:19) The difference between a false Christian and a true Christian is that a true Christian doesn't just believe in God, he *knows* God personally. In order to truly know someone, we must spend time with that person. If you have no desire to spend time with God through prayer and learn more about him through reading his Word, you should consider whether you really *know* him.

Believes in Self—Some people think they are Christians because they strive to live a moral life. They assess themselves as "good" in comparison to others. Based on their good deeds, they believe they have earned the right to enter Heaven. The Bible teaches that our good deeds will not purchase our ticket to Heaven: "all our righteous acts are like filthy rags." (Isa. 64:6) If we could receive salvation by being a good person, then God sent his son to die for no reason. To say that you are good enough to enter Heaven on your own is to reject the atoning sacrifice of Jesus Christ.

Believes in Religion—Being a Christian is not about a *religion*, it's about a *relationship*. Salvation is not found in attending church three out of four Sunday services a month. Salvation is not found in your denominational preference. Salvation is found in the person of Jesus Christ. Going to church, wiping noses in the church nursery, and teaching a Sunday school class does not win you brownie points in the Lamb's Book of Life. The Lord condemned the "religious" leaders and all their religious rituals when He said, "These people come near to me with their mouth and honor me with their lips, but their hearts are far from me. Their worship of me is made up only of rules taught by men." (Isa. 29:13) Jesus described such people as those who washed the outside of the cup while the inside was still unclean (Matt. 23:25). God is concerned with your heart, not with your outward religion.

Believes in Unconditioned Mercy—I wish I had a quarter for every time I have heard, "God is too good to send me to hell. His mercy will prevail." It is true that God is merciful, but He is also perfectly just. He is too holy to just "write off" our sin; the penalty must be paid. For those who *accept* his son, God's justice falls on Jesus, and they receive mercy. But for those who *reject* his Son, God's justice falls on them. Jesus explains it this way: "Whoever acknowledges me before men, I will also acknowledge him before my Father in Heaven. But whoever disowns me before men, I will disown him before my Father in Heaven." (Matt. 10:32-33)

God's justice and mercy find their ultimate expression on the cross, where Jesus died as an atonement for our sins. By pouring out his wrath on Jesus, he pours out his mercy on those who believe. But those who reject his mercy by rejecting his son will most definitely suffer his wrath. Jesus said, "Whoever believes in him is not condemned, but whoever does not believe stands condemned already because he has not believed in the name of God's one and only son." (John 3:18)

A True Christian

Becoming a Christian is as simple as receiving a gift. In fact, salvation is a free gift. We cannot earn it. We cannot buy it. Jesus bought it for us with his own blood. He paid our debt in full so that we do not have to pay for it ourselves. Paul says, "the wages of sin is death, but the gift of God is eternal life." (Rom. 6:23). In other words, the "wages," or consequence, of our sins is death. The Bible defines eternal death as being separated from God (see Matt. 7:23). A true Christian:

Believes He is a Sinner—"For all have sinned and fall short of the glory of God." (Rom. 3:23) Sin is what separates us from God. Sin is simply breaking God's law, his commandments, such as lying. We have all broken God's law. Therefore, we are all sinners.

Believes Jesus Christ Died for Him—"For God so loved the world that he gave his one and only Son, that whoever believes in him shall not perish but have eternal life." (John 3:16) There is no greater love than the love that Jesus has for you. It wasn't the nails that held him to the cross that day, but his love for you. He suffered and died in order that you might have life abundantly.

Because God is holy, he cannot tolerate sin. In fact, he said that all sin must be punished by death. In all fairness, we should each pay for our own sins. But God, out of his love for us, paid the price when he sent Jesus to die on the cross. God called this Christ's "atonement," or payment, for our sins.

Believes Salvation is Only Through Jesus Christ—Jesus says, "I am the way and the truth and the life. No one comes to the Father except through me" (John 14:6). Jesus Christ is the one and only provision for our sinfulness. In order for us to be forgiven, there has to be atonement for our sins. Jesus is our atonement. He died so that we might live. He paid the price so that we do not have to: "For Christ died for sins once and for all, the righteous for the unrighteous, to bring you to God" (1 Peter 3:18).

Believes in God's Promise—"Yet to all who received him, to those who believed in his name, he gave the right to become children of God" (John 1:12). God's Word is holy and true. If you acknowledge yourself as a sinner, if you believe that Jesus died on the cross for your sins, if you repent of your sins and invite Jesus to be your Lord and Savior, you will be saved. Jesus promised, "Here I am! I stand at the door and knock. If anyone hears my voice and opens the door, I will come in" (Rev. 3:20).

Becoming a Christian

If you would like to accept Jesus as your Savior, receive God's forgiveness, and have the assurance of eternal life with him in Heaven, I invite you to speak to God with this prayer:

Dear Father in Heaven, I acknowledge that I am a sinner in need of your mercy, forgiveness, and grace. I believe that Jesus died for me, paying the price for my sins. I believe Jesus rose from the dead, conquering death in order for me to live eternally. I am sorry for my sins against you. Please forgive me. Please wash away my sins with the precious blood you shed for me. I invite you to come into my life and reign as my Lord and Savior. Help me to know you. Help me to obey you. Thank you, Jesus, for saving me and for giving me new life in you. Amen

Everyone who calls on the name of the Lord will be saved.

(Rom. 10:13)

B

How to Lead Your Child to Christ

A ll Christian parents long for the day their child receives Jesus Christ as Lord and Savior. "Mommy, I asked Jesus to be my Savior," brings tears to our eyes and joy to our hearts. As parents desiring God's abundant life for our children, we should be overjoyed to hear those words. However, as wise shepherds over the hearts of our children, we should be very cautious.

Leading our children to Christ involves much more than guiding them in a simple prayer. It's living an example before them of what it means to walk with Christ on a daily basis. It's teaching them God's viewpoint in every situation. It's demonstrating forgiveness. It's asking forgiveness. It's living, breathing, and adoring the Word of God in the presence of your children, as well as in their absence.

Parents must be careful not to offer their children a premature assurance of their salvation. It's normal to hope for our children's salvation. Yet, we must not allow our hopefulness to hold on to simple words from their mouths that do not reflect a change in their hearts. We must not let our desire for peace of mind deceive or mislead our children into a false sense of salvation.

A well-respected pastor once stated that he could lead almost any child under the age of ten to make a profession of faith in Christ. This pastor wasn't boasting in his abilities. He was making a point about the naiveté of children. A child can be easily deceived about the state of his soul. Most children will respond to a smooth-talking, convincing adult with very little prompting. However, a mere profession is very different from a true conversion. A profession is declaring your faith. A conversion is demonstrating or living out your faith. Profession is "talking the talk." Conversion is "walking the walk."

Children who grow up in church have witnessed the power of God in the lives of others. They trust in their parent's confidence that God is real. They have listened to the truths of God's Word preached from the pulpit Sunday after Sunday. Is it any wonder that they would *believe* in God and know exactly how to profess that belief? It is a dangerous assumption that your child is truly saved simply because he has a knowledge of the Scriptures and professes his belief in God. It is foolish to offer assurance to a child based on knowledge alone.

Understanding the naiveté of children, the hopefulness of parents, and the crafty schemes of the great deceiver can help us remain sober-minded and keep us from risking the tender souls of our precious children.

Am I saying that a child cannot experience a true conversion? Certainly not. I am saying that we must be very careful to consider the intellectual immaturity of children and how that plays a part in their readiness to understand and receive Christ.

Am I saying that we should put them off each time they speak of salvation and baptism, telling them to wait until they are older? Absolutely not. We must urge them to come to Christ *now* and not delay. A heart that rejects the prompting of the Holy Spirit can become hardened to responding in the future. We must encourage them to recognize the temptation to "think about accepting Christ later." To put off trusting in Jesus as Savior and Lord allows the devil time to weave his wicked web around the hearts of our children, tightening his grip as he sucks out all the tenderness.

Encourage Your Child—When your child speaks of his love and commitment to Jesus, let him know that you are overjoyed by his desire to please God. Encourage him to discuss his thoughts and ask you questions about things that confuse him. Encourage him to get to know Jesus better by spending time with the Lord in prayer and by reading his Word. You may want to consider letting him pick out an age-appropriate Bible and devotional book (there are some available for beginning readers). When he initiates time with God, let him know that you are happy to see him seeking Jesus.

Never discourage your child by saying, "If you really knew God, you wouldn't act like that!" To say such a thing would dishearten your child and render you a hypocrite. As a sinner, you fall equally as short of the glory of God and need his grace as much as any. Resist the temptation to use God's wrath as a threat to try to correct your child's behavior: "God's going to get you if you don't quit fighting with your sister!" Encourage him to approach God's throne of grace through love of virtue, not fear of punishment.

When he sins, encourage him to find refuge in the forgiveness of Jesus. Let him witness you do the same. Teach your sons and daughters the Biblical model of admitting sin, being truly sorry for sin, asking forgiveness, and changing sinful behaviors and attitudes.

Challenge Your Child—Tell him that God defines true commitment as never turning back. Inform him that turning to Christ is a lifelong commitment, not a one-time prayer. Explain that his commitment must not be based on the commitment of his parents or friends. Tell him that his commitment must be so strong and true that even if those he loves and those who love him turn away from God, he must not.

Ask him questions that do not require a yes or no answer. For example: "How do you know God loves you?" "Why do you need a Savior?" "What has God done about your sin?" Do not prompt, hint, or put words in his mouth. Allowing him to answer the questions on his own will help you discern his level of understanding and spiritual readiness. If you determine your child is ready to receive Christ as his Savior and Lord, refer to Appendix A, "How to become a Christian."

Look for Evidence of Conversion—One definition of repentance is "to change one's mind." A true conversion is demonstrated by turning from sin to God, regardless of the age of the one converted. If your child has truly been converted there will be a visible difference in him. If the Spirit of Christ truly dwells in his heart, the character of Christ will flow from his heart. In watching for signs of your child's conversion, ask yourself: Does he try to apply God's Word to his life?

Does he desire to obey his parents/authority more than before?

Does he seem hungry to know Jesus?

Does he receive correction and instruction with humility?

Does he have a strong interest in pleasing God?

Does he seem to genuinely love Jesus?

Do you see a difference in him?

How to Pray for Your Child

No matter what stage of life our children are in, the most important thing we can do is to pray for them. Whether they're in diapers, danger, love, rebellion, or a sports car, our most powerful and effective tool in parenting is fervent prayer over every aspect of their lives.

As parents cursed with a sin nature, we are bound to mess up. We will make some wrong decisions. From time to time we will lose our temper—or shall I say, we will *find* it! Because we are not perfect, we will let our children down, set poor examples, and fail them in more ways than one. However, there is one thing that will always reap fruit and never return void. We can pray for our children in accordance with God's Word. Stormie Omartian says, "Being a perfect parent doesn't matter. Being a praying parent does."

To pray for our children directly from God's Word is to pray in harmony with God's perfect will for their lives. It is to bind up our shallow and vain desires and unleash the wisdom and power of our mighty Lord. When we pray from God's Word, we surrender our foolish misconceptions of what is best by acknowledging that God's ways are not our ways. To pray from the Scriptures is to seek the will of the Father rather than the will of the parent. "For my thoughts are not your thoughts, neither are your ways my ways," declares the Lord. "As the heavens are higher than the earth, so are my ways higher than your ways and my thoughts than your thoughts" (Isa. 55:8–9).

Why should we pray?

Prayer is a command of God—"Be joyful always; pray continually; giving thanks to God in all circumstances, for this is God's will for you in Christ Jesus" (1 Thess. 5:16–18).

Prayer draws us near to God—"What other nation is so great as to have their gods near them the way the Lord our God is near us whenever we pray to him?" (Deut. 4:7).

Prayer releases God's power—"Therefore confess your sins to each other and pray for each other so that you may be healed. The prayer of a righteous man is powerful and effective" (James 5:16).

What should we pray?

1. Pray that our children would come to salvation through faith in Jesus Christ.

   1 Timothy 2:3–4

2. Pray that they would honor and obey us as their parents as well as those in authority over them.

   Ephesians 6:1–3
   Hebrews 13:17

3. Pray that the Lord would surround them with godly friends and role models.

148

1 Corinthians 15:33
Proverbs 13:20
Proverbs 27:17

4. Pray that the Lord would implant into their hearts a hunger and thirst for him.

Psalm 42:1–2

5. Pray that the Lord would give them the Spirit of wisdom and revelation so that they might know him better.

Ephesians 1:17

6. Pray that the eyes of their hearts would always be enlightened in order that they might know the hope to which he has called them.

Ephesians 1:18

7. Pray that they would always follow the truth and reject the lies of Satan.

Proverbs 22:3
Titus 2:11–12

8. Pray that they would bear much fruit for God's glory.

Galatians 5:22–23
Ephesians 2:10
1 John 3:16–18

9. Pray that they would flee temptation.

1 Corinthians 10:13
2 Timothy 2:22–26

10. Pray that they would use their gifts and talents to honor the Lord.

Proverbs 16:3
1 Corinthians 10:31

11. Pray that they would have freedom from fear as they trust in the Lord.

Psalm 56:13
2 Thessalonians 3:16
2 Timothy 1:7

12. Pray that they would keep themselves sexually pure for their future mates.

1 Corinthians 10:8
Hebrews 13:4

13. Pray that the Lord would bring godly mates into their lives.

2 Corinthians 6:14–16

14. Pray that they would take captive every thought and make it obedient to Christ.

2 Corinthians 10:5
Philippians 4:8

15. Pray that they would become more like him.

Romans 8:28–29

In every situation, we must learn to trust in the Lord and lean not on our own understanding . . . and we all know that with children, there are going to be some situations! We must realize that every blessing, every trial, and every heart-breaking event has been filtered through his hands of love. We must have full confidence in God's sovereignty.

How should we pray?

Study your children and know what is going on in their lives so you will know how to pray specifically for each one of them. Find verses from God's Word relating to the issues they are facing. Ask your children how you can pray for them. Pray the Word of God for your children (Hebrews 4:12).

Pray out loud with them. Pray often. Pray conversationally as though you are talking to someone in the room with you (without a lot of "thees" and "thous" or churchy-sounding phrases that are hard for children to understand). Pray everywhere—indoors, outdoors, driving in the car, feeding the cat—so your child realizes his Heavenly Father is always available.

Pray about little things (like a lost toy) as well as big things (like Daddy's lost job). Tell them of God's faithfulness in answering your prayers on their behalf. Consider recording your answered prayers in a journal for them to read in years to come.

Prayer will not only draw you closer to God, but it will draw you closer to your children. Encourage your children to pray about everything. Assure them that God will faithfully meet their every need!

Notes

Chapter 1

1. Mabel Bartlett and Sophia Baker, *Mothers—Makers of Men* (New York: Exposition Press, 1952), 92.

2. Louis M. Notkin, ed., *Mother Tributes from the World's Great Literature* (New York: Samuel Curl, 1943), 177.

3. Lindsey O'Conner, *Moms Who Changed the World* (Eugene, OR.: Harvest House, 1999), 65

Chapter 2

1. Tedd Tripp, *Shepherding a Child's Heart* (Wapwallopen, PA: Shepherd Press, 1995), 20.

Chapter 3

1. Ibid, 21.

Chapter 5

1. Much of the material in this section is a reworking of the excellent material in Lou Priolo's *The Heart of Anger*, (New York: Calvary Press, 1997) particularly chapter 4.

2. Lou Priolo, *The Heart of Anger* (New York: Calvary Press, 1997), 64–65.

3. Ibid., 65–66.

4. Ibid., 66 This entire example is borrowed from Lou Priolo. I have simply substituted my common place shoe-tying for a different example. Mothers tie a lot of shoes before their children learn.

Chapter 7

1. Ibid., 125. In this chapter I have borrowed a great deal from chapters 9 and 10 of Lou Priolo's *The Heart of Anger*.

Chapter 8

1. I am again indebted to Lou Priolo for much of this material.

2. H. Clay Trumbull, *Hints on Child Training* (Eugene, OR: Great Expectations, 1990), 129, 130, 131.

3. Ginger Plowman, *Wise Words for Moms* (Wapwallopen, PA: Shepherd Press, 2001).

Chapter 9

1. Tedd Tripp, *Shepherding a Child's Heart* (Wapwallopen, PA: Shepherd Press, 1995), 130.

Chapter 10

1. "Of course, while the Bible does give us instructions on how to live, it's so much more than that! It's a huge sweeping story told in narrative, law, poetry, prophecy, song, letter, vision, etc., telling us where history began and where it's going—and above all, WHO history is all about!"—Walter Henegar.

2. Roy Lessin, *Spanking: Why, When, How* (Minneapolis, MN: Bethany House, 1979), 18.

3. Roy Lessin, *Spanking—A Loving Discipline* (Minneapolis, MN: Bethany House, 2002), 60.

4. Ibid, 61.

5. Ibid, 61.

6. Ibid, 62.

7. Bruce Ray, *Withhold Not Correction* (Phillipsburg, NJ: Presbyterian & Reformed Publishing Company, 1978), 103.

8. Tedd Tripp, *Shepherding a Child's Heart* (Wapwallopen, PA: Shepherd Press, 1995), 137.

Chapter 11

1. Roy Lessin, *Spanking—A Loving Discipline* (Minneapolis, MN: Bethany House, 2002), 50–51.

2. Ibid, 53.

3. Ibid, 56–57.

4. Bruce Ray, *Withhold Not Correction* (Phillipsburg, NJ: Presbyterian & Reformed Publishing Company, 1978), 105.

5. Ibid, 106.

Chapter 12

1. Roy Lessin, *Spanking—A Loving Discipline* (Minneapolis, MN: Bethany House, 2002), 27.

Vist Shepherd Press

On Facebook: Just seach for *Shepherd Press*
Our Website: www.Shepherdpress.com
Our Blog: http://www.shepherdpress.com/blog/

Shepherd Press BookTweets:
Broken Down House: @BDHouse
Get Outta My Face: @outtamy
When Sinners Say "I Do": @WSSID

Six Week Study Guide
"Don't Make Me Count to Three!"

Dive deeper into God's Word with this six-week study guide designed to strengthen understanding of heart-oriented discipline from a biblical perspective. Ideal for personal or group study, this Guide takes you through very practical applications of Scripture for parenting and gives you heart-probing questions for reflection for your own growth as a mom.

Available at Amazon or Shepherd Press

Wise Words for Moms
iPhone, iPad App

Take *Wise Words for Moms* with you everywhere!
My child is complaining…or fearful…or selfish. How do I help him?
Wise Words for Moms lists heart-searching questions to ask your child, then directs you to Scriptures with God's encouragements for change.

Features:
• Link to ESV or *YouVersion* Bible
• Note jotting capability
• Add scripture passages you find

Available at Apple App Store

Parenting Resources

Heart of Anger by Lou Priolo is a resource manual for parents whose children struggle with anger. If you are a parent who is concerned that you may have an angry kid, or one in the making, this book will offer real help and hope.

Teach Them Diligently by Lou Priolo is about how to use the Scriptures to train your children. "Teach Them Diligently holds a wealth of practical and biblical advice for parents seeking to fulfill the mandate of Deuteronomy 6:6-7."— John MacArthur

Shepherding a Child's Heart by Tedd Tripp teaches you how to speak to the heart of your child. Written for parents of any age, this insightful book provides perspectives and procedures for shepherding your child's heart into the paths of life.

Devotional materials for Children

Herein is Love: a series for children by Nancy Ganz—Beginning with creation, Nancy moves through the Old Testament narrative with warmth and keen insights, bringing these stories to life. Each book includes the Biblical account in story form and a Teacher's Guide that includes memory work, craft ideas, review questions, songs, and outdoor activities. Currently available: Genesis, Exodus, and Leviticus. Nancy is currently working on the rest of the series that includes Numbers, Deuteronomy and Joshua.

The Gospel for Children by John Leuzarder is an excellent tool to aid Christian parents in teaching the essentials of the Gospel to their youngsters. Each point is accompanied by Scripture references and an illustration to facilitate memory.

The Young Peacemaker by Corlette Sande is a twelve lesson curriculum that teaches biblical peacemaking. Topics include: What conflict is, How to avoid conflict, and How to respond to conflict. The Young Peacemaker includes a 200 page teacher's manual and each lesson is accompanied by a 10 page student activity book.